Dear Tony

Happy birthday! May

feel Hashem's blessing in all of

life's experiences

Shaul Rosenblatt

FINDING LIGHT IN THE DARKNESS

Finding Light in the Darkness

The Toughest Challenges and How to Grow from Them

SHAUL ROSENBLATT

A TARGUM PRESS BOOK

First published 2006

ISBN 1-56871-412-2

Published by:
TARGUM PRESS, INC.
22700 W. Eleven Mile Rd.
Southfield, MI 48034
E-mail: targum@targum.com
Fax: 888-298-9992
www.targum.com

Distributed by:
FELDHEIM PUBLISHERS
208 Airport Executive Park
Nanuet, NY 10954

Printing plates by Frank, Jerusalem
Printed in Israel by Chish

Jerusalem
June 13, 2006

Shaul Rosenblatt has written a book that is personal, deeply moving, and deeply wise. It is extremely enjoyable and readable while being profoundly insightful. I think it will be greatly meaningful and helpful to anyone grappling with life's challenges.

I highly recommend for everyone to read this book.

Noah Weinberg
Rabbi Noah Weinberg

American Friends of Yeshiva Aish HaTorah, Inc.
400 South Lake Drive • Lakewood, NJ 08701-3167 • Tel: 732-364-6683 • Fax: 732-875-0576 • Email: info@aish.com
Tax ID# (EIN): 51-0243498 • Exemption granted pursuant to section 501(c)(3) of the Internal Revenue Code

For Elana

Thank you
for filling my world
with light.

Contents

Acknowledgments

Many people have helped make this book possible and I would like to express my appreciation to:

The generous sponsors of the book – Mark and Gabriella Addlestone, Bernie and Marilyn Dexter, Nic Hai, James Hyman, Daniel and Valeria Levy, and Adrian and Laura Weller.

Shoshana Lepon, who put a tremendous amount of work into making the initial edit.

My rebbe, Rabbi Noah Weinberg, who taught me, and continues to teach me, the foundations of everything I know.

Rebbetzin Dena Weinberg, whose *tznius* will not allow me to say too much, but if it did, I probably couldn't say enough.

My parents, who gave me life, a loving family, and a warm home from which to build my own.

Joanne and Irwin Asher, who have been wonderful in-laws and grandparents through very difficult times.

Rabbi Yissachar and Esther Granitsky, who have always been behind Chana in all that she has done.

Family, friends, and community who have all been so incredibly supportive all along the way.

And of course, to my wife Chana, who has encouraged me, supported me, and advised me throughout. You picked us up when we were lost and helped us to find ourselves again.

Thank You, Hashem, for blessing me with the publishing of this book.

Preface

F*inding Light in the Darkness* is about the mechanisms I developed — both together with my wife Elana, *z"l*, and subsequently, alone — that helped us deal with incredibly challenging circumstances. I am hoping that the lessons I learned will be of help to others who are facing difficulty. We all go through pain in our lives. No one is exempt. What makes some people different from others is how they rise to the challenge of their pain. I hope to share some tools that the reader may find of value.

Rabbi Shaul Rosenblatt

Introduction

A MATCH MADE IN HEAVEN?

The first time I met Elana, she was eighteen and I was twenty-two. We were both *madrichim* for Aish HaTorah on an outreach program called Discovery, in Jerusalem. It was a match made in heaven — sort of.

As I was waiting in the lobby of the Discovery Center one morning, I glanced over and saw someone come into the room who was dressed like a schoolgirl and seemed even younger. Why was she here? She looked religious, so she couldn't be a participant in the program. And surely Moshe, the program director, could not have hired her as a *madrichah*? How could this Orthodox little girl relate to the secular worldly people in their twenties and thirties who would be passing through our doors?

I immediately went to clear up the matter with Moshe. "Yes, she is a *madrichah*," he told me.

"Well, then, fire her!" I shot back. "We are a professional

organization, trying to reach young Jews who don't relate to Judaism. This girl just doesn't have what it takes." My appeals, fortuitously, did not make a dent.

Elana didn't notice me that day, but two days later we had a *kumzitz*, a gathering around a bonfire. Someone brought a guitar and everyone sang along. She looked over at me and noticed me for the first time. Her thoughts were not wildly different than mine. "He can't be a participant because of the black yarmulke that he wears. But he's swigging beer out of a bottle and smoking a cigarette. How could Aish hire such a lowlife to be a counselor?!"

As I said, a match made in heaven...

We were assigned to work on the same program, so eventually we had to speak to one another. And when we did, I actually enjoyed the conversation. As the days and weeks of summer progressed, I found myself talking to Elana more and more. Discovery was an Orthodox program and counselors did not socialize, but somehow, we managed to find excuses to talk about issues that were, of course, absolutely crucial to the running of the program.

I found myself really liking Elana. But it just couldn't be. She was right out of high school — so naive. She wasn't classical "*rebbetzin* material" — and I was soon going to be a rabbi. But the more I tried to avoid her, the more we seemed to meet. I was surprised at myself. She was taller than me. She was quiet and soft spoken — so unlike myself. She was one of those sweet and innocent FFB's that we BT's didn't even think about and she was such a goodie-goodie — and how I hated goodie-goodies! I couldn't figure out what I liked about her, but we managed to talk for hours on end without running out of things to say.

I wasn't marriage-minded at the time, so I didn't think of her as someone whom I might date. But I did have a friend, Avi, who had been unsuccessfully dating for quite a while. As time went on and I thought more and more about Elana, it occurred to me that it might be a good idea to set them up. Still, I didn't want to set my friend up with a girl I'd just had a few conversations with, so I started making inquiries — as is usual in the Orthodox world. The more people I asked, the more I was impressed. I didn't hear anything negative from anyone, only amazing praise. She was just too good to be true. I said to myself, *I know I'm a good friend, but why am I setting Avi up with her? Even though I'm not quite ready to date, shouldn't I go out with her myself?*

I asked Rabbi Appel, the senior rabbi at Discovery, if he would find out whether or not she was dating. He got on the case immediately and she told him she had not started dating yet, but who did he have in mind? "Why are you asking if you're not dating yet?" he asked. "Well, I'm not dating, but if it happens to be Shaul (or Stevie as I was known then), maybe I might reconsider..."

Rabbi Appel came back to me to tell me we were going out Wednesday night. I put up a brave fight. I protested that I had only asked him to find out if she had started dating, not to organize a date! We argued back and forth, but in the end, I very reluctantly acquiesced.

Wednesday came and Elana acted as if nothing had changed. At the Discovery program that day, she didn't blink an eye. She didn't look at me, she didn't smile, she didn't even glance in my direction. I figured Rabbi Appel must be pulling a fast one on me. Was I really going out with her that evening?

Finally, the day was almost over. I couldn't wait any longer. She went into the counselors' room and I followed. I found her looking for something in a cupboard. Sensing my presence, she slowly closed the cupboard doors, looked me straight in the eye, and smiled at me for the first time — a smile that would be her hallmark for as long as I knew her, even during her darkest hours; a smile of such goodness, such sweetness that I knew right there and then that if I were lucky enough to marry her, I would be truly blessed. "I'll be ready in ten minutes," she said, still smiling, as she walked out of the room.

After the first date, neither of us had any doubts. We got along so well! We had similar goals, similar values, similar dreams — similar everything. And we had such fun together. We were like teenagers who couldn't stop giggling the whole night. I guess, to be fair, Elana actually was a teenager.

We went out six times in seven days because Elana was returning to America after that. At the end of our last date, we knew it was too early to get officially engaged, but each of us clearly knew

Elana and I at our vort in 1989.

that it was going to happen. Three months later, after finishing my rabbinic degree, I went to America and we got engaged. The only way we could describe the whole process — and we quoted it again and again and again — was a verse from Psalms: "I will sing to God for He has bestowed His goodness upon me." It was all so right and so perfect. It seemed to us that stories like this only happened in fairy tales, not in real life. We kept pinching ourselves to make sure that we were not dreaming.

Elana finished her year at university and I came to America for the wedding. The *chuppah* part of our wedding video focuses on me taking tissue after tissue from my father to wipe away my tears of joy. I was so happy. I was marrying, not the girl of my boyhood dreams, but the girl with whom I could create new and more mature dreams — a *bas Yisrael* in the deepest sense of the word.

Elana and I sharing a joke at our wedding.

Every day, I wake up in the morning and thank God for Elana. She was a wonderful dream — all too fleeting a dream — but a wonderful dream nevertheless.

I will not bore you with the details of our life until Rosh HaShanah 1998. We set up home in Jerusalem, then moved to England to set up Aish HaTorah UK. We had four beautiful children — each of whom reminds me of Elana in his or her own special way. We had our ups and downs, as all marriages do, but generally we found more happiness in our relationship than we had ever imagined existed.

The summer of 1998 was a particularly difficult one for us. We had our last two children quite close to each other and so we had two babies in the house. I remember our whole family going to America in August. Neither of the babies had a seat, so Elana and I sat on opposite sides of the aisle. As the flight was beginning its descent, one of the babies threw up over the armrest. The other baby, on the opposite side, took one look and threw up also. The plane was going down, so the vomit started rolling down the aisle. Everyone had their seatbelts fastened, including the stewardesses, so all we could do was sit there and watch. Needless to say, we were not the most popular people on the flight!

Having two children who were babies at the same time started to become overwhelming for us. We started to feel challenged by our circumstances — perhaps a little frustrated even. Life was not going the way we wanted it to. But that was nothing compared to what was to come next.

Elana first felt the lump right before our trip. She was twenty-seven years old and nursing a baby. We just didn't think it could be serious. Surely people don't get cancer at this age. But they do.

We went to the doctor as soon as we returned from America, and he said it was surely just an infected milk duct. "Come back in two weeks if it hasn't gone away." And come back we did...a few days before Rosh HaShanah. The lump had not gone away; it had grown bigger — quite a bit bigger. And now she had a lump in her neck, as well. The doctor was still sure it was an infection, but he sent us to see a surgeon just to put our mind at rest for the holidays. We went right after Rosh HaShanah. The surgeon was very nice. He asked for the details and gave us one small bit of reassurance — reassurance that later on we certainly could have done without. He told us that it could not be cancer because cancer could not possibly grow as fast as this lump had.

He said he would do a mammogram just in case.

The doctor in charge of the mammogram did an ultrasound first. She said that she did not know what it was, but it did not look like cancer. She was about to send us home when I suggested the mammogram that we had been sent for in the first place. "Why not?" she said. "It can't do any harm!"

The mammogram was the first time we started to seriously worry. Once the doctor had started looking, she wanted to look at another angle and another and another. She kept us in the X-ray room for almost an hour. Then she disappeared. I searched and discovered her hiding place, wanting to make sure she still thought it wasn't cancer. Suddenly she got very professional with me. She could not give me results; I had to refer to our surgeon. But could she at least put our minds at rest before the weekend? I asked. She would send her results to the surgeon and we would see him on Monday. And that was that.

The next couple of days were tense. It was a painful weekend and we were both on edge.

We got the surgeon's office early in the morning and he kept us waiting for over an hour and a half. He seemed to be looking for anything and everything he could possibly do rather than see us.

Finally, very reluctantly, he called us in to his office. And as soon as he did, we knew what he had in store for us.

"It's malignant," was all he said.

"Are you sure? Could it be a mistake? Is there any other possibility?"

We were desperate to cling to any straw.

But there were to be no straws.

Elana had primary breast cancer, with secondaries in her lymph nodes and both lungs. Given the limitations of modern medicine at that time and still today, that was tantamount to a death sentence — a slow death sentence, perhaps, but a sure one, nonetheless.

For almost three years we battled together, grew together, lived our days together to their fullest until, in August of 2001, Elana passed away. That beautiful girl who had first smiled that wonderful smile at me all those years before; the girl who had given me four beautiful children; the girl who had never been sick — had always been so robust and healthy — until she got cancer; the girl who I had never, ever heard say a bad word about another human being; the wonderful *bas Yisrael* with whom I was so desperate to spend the rest of my life. Gone... Gone... Forever... She had left me a widower; left me with four young children, alone to face the world.

This book is about growing through pain. Elana and I spent a tremendous amount of time and energy trying to ensure that our experience of her illness was a uniformly positive one — which it was. We developed a lot of ideas and mechanisms for overcoming challenge and I share them in the hope that others will find them as valuable as we did.

Elana

I want to share a few stories about Elana. I'm not just indulging — I truly believe that others might find her as inspirational as I and many around her did. I have a book that people wrote in during the shivah and so many people said that they could only describe her as an angel. She was not an angel. As her husband, I knew all her shortcomings. But if anyone I know came close, it was certainly Elana.

During her last days, she was so sick. Cancer is an incredibly horrific disease — for those of you who have been with a loved one in the final stages of cancer, you know what I mean. (And for

Elana with our four children.

those of you who have not, I pray that you should never have to do so.) She was as thin as a rake. She was in a great deal of pain. She could not keep much down in the way of food, but worst of all was her breathing. She felt constantly as though she was suffocating. And suffocating she was, with the cancer slowly filling up the space of both her lungs. Over and over again, I would ask her how she was doing. Over and over again — without any exception at all — she would smile her beautiful smile at me and say that she was doing great. It was not a show. She really was doing great.

Even though we had twenty-four-hour-a-day nursing care for Elana's final six weeks, a Jewish nurse from the community would often come around just to make sure everything was in order. One time, she walked over on Shabbat and spent a couple of hours checking things out. Finally, she said good-bye to Elana and began to leave. Elana suddenly panicked and didn't want her to go. It now took her about ten minutes to catch enough breath to speak even a few words, but she motioned me to come over. I was very anxious to hear what was distressing her so. Finally, gathering all her energy to speak, she was able to whisper in my ear. Amidst all her pain, Elana had noticed that it was raining outside and that the nurse did not have a proper coat. She insisted that the nurse take her own coat so she would not get wet on her way home.

This concern for others even in the midst of her own tragedy was one of Elana's hallmarks.

On her final Shabbat in this world, we had guests over. They were discussing our china and I told them it was thirty years old. Elana immediately whispered to her sister to say that it is still made today. I was surprised that Elana should be concerned to point out that her china was not out of date until her sister explained to me that this was not her point. Elana had told her that she did not want the guests to be worried about breaking or chipping something that was irreplaceable.

I regularly felt humbled in her presence.

We knew from the outset that the cancer was in her lungs and so, having spent many a late night on the Internet, I realized that a cough was a very bad sign. During the three years of her illness, she would occasionally start coughing, and I would always be terrified until it went away. During her final months, she developed a cough that just wouldn't go away. I think that we both knew deep down that it wasn't going to.

She started to act rather strangely during this period and it was only later on that I realized why. Very often, we would be in a room together and suddenly she would run out for a moment. Even midconversation, she would say she had to step out quickly, and she would return a moment later. At the time it seemed strange. But as the weeks went on, I understood that she was leaving the room to cough, because she knew how much it scared me to hear it. The trouble she went to so that I wouldn't hear her cough was quite unbelievable.

In the end, she could no longer keep up the pretense, and I realized that her cough had gotten much worse than I thought, but she had been doing a very good job of thinking of me and concealing her pain. Most people, I believe, would have wanted their spouse's sympathy and support, but Elana was willing to bear her own pain privately and alone in order to spare me from mine.

As I said, I don't remember ever hearing a bad word from her mouth about another person. A childhood friend attended the shivah from America. He said the same. He never heard a bad word about anyone from her. Even when she knew something about someone that I wanted to know, she would refuse to tell me and was extremely careful not to hint at anything either. If I began to guess, she would go so far as to make up stories to mislead me. If I was trying to get something out of her, she would just refuse to talk to me, in case she carelessly gave something away that might be detrimental about someone else. And when she wanted to be stubborn about this, she was very stubborn!

When she left for America after we had been going out for our first week, she accidentally left her diary in my apartment. Here was my opportunity to see what she really felt about me. To see what was really going on in her mind. I knew I shouldn't, but it was such a temptation that I could not resist. I found it full of sincere love. Later that day there was a message from her on my answer machine. She was desperate to get a hold of me before she left, to tell me about the diary, so she had called a number of times from the airport. She said she knew that I would be unable to resist reading it and she wanted to get to me before I did to tell me that I could, so that I would do so with her permission as opposed to without.

Another example of her greatness was when she was in labor. She was clearly in tremendous pain during each contraction. She wanted a natural labor, so she took no form of pain relief. Even during a contraction when she was virtually holding back from screaming, she would look over at me and say she wasn't really in pain, it just looked like it. She said that she knew it hurt me more to see her in pain than it did for her to be in pain and I should not worry because things were not what they seemed to be.

She had no concern for herself — even at a time when she had every right to. She was only concerned about me. It wasn't about her pain, it was about my pain at seeing her in pain. That's all she worried about. To her, seeing someone else in pain was infinitely worse than feeling her own pain and she assumed that everyone else felt the same way. Selflessness was so completely natural to her that she could not imagine someone relating to the world differently.

Our second child, Shifra, was born on seder night. Elana insisted on doing the seder in the delivery room in between contractions. She would calm down from the contraction and say, "Okay, let's drink the second cup of wine now" or "Let's eat the matzah" or "Quickly, let's read some more of the Haggadah before the next one comes." We made it as far as the *afikoman* before she gave

Elana holding Shifra.

birth and only then did she decide that now her priority lay with her newborn baby, not the seder.

During the difficult years of Elana's illness, we had a young, non-Jewish, Romanian cleaning lady help out in the house a couple of times a week. Her name was Michaela.

On numerous occasions, I came home and found Michaela and Elana deep in conversation. Sometimes Michaela had tears in her eyes. When I asked Elana what was going on, she would tell me that she was advising Michaela on her relationship with her boyfriend or her parents or the difficulties she was encountering getting permission to remain in England.

If I asked for more details, Elana would always decline. Michaela had confided in her privately, and I knew there was no point in even trying to get it out of her. In Elana's shivah book, Michaela wrote that she looked up to Elana as a mother.

No one was beneath her, no one was unworthy of her attention. If there was another human being in need — even a cleaning lady whom she was paying to work, not to chat — she would drop everything and be there.

Finally, when eulogizing her on the thirtieth day of her passing, Rabbi Noah Weinberg said that it's not everyone who can do a kindness at their own funeral. Let me explain.

Her funeral was on August 9, 2001. You might recognize the date. The funeral was due to be held at 10 a.m. in Jerusalem, but for some reason, our flight from London was delayed by two hours. There was a strange electrical fault on the plane, and they took everyone off the plane and told us the flight was canceled and the next flight would be in twelve hours. Then they suddenly found the solution and told everyone to board the plane. Some passengers had already taken buses to a hotel for the night, but the airline personnel brought them back.

Since the flight was delayed two hours, so was the funeral. Instead of being held at 10 a.m., it was called for 12:00 that afternoon and lasted until around 2 p.m. Two of our students from Aish in England had planned to go to the funeral at 10 a.m. and then have lunch at a restaurant called Sbarro's in Jerusalem. They planned to meet at the restaurant at 1:30 p.m. Due to the delay of the funeral, their lunch meeting was canceled. That afternoon, at around 2 p.m., a suicide bomber walked into Sbarro's and blew himself up, killing fifteen innocent Jews. Had the funeral not been delayed, these two students would likely have been among the victims. I'm no Kabbalist, and I'm not usually into these types of things, but I certainly feel that Elana had a hand in this.

(You may ask at this point — as probably you should — yes, but what about the people who did die in the bombing? Didn't God look after them, as well? This type of question is, of course, the whole purpose of this book and I hope that the later chapters will go a long way to giving you a deeper understanding.)

A few months after Elana's passing, someone who knew her told me that he had spoken to a Kabbalist about her. As I said, I'm not so into Kabbalists myself, but what he said was interesting. He said that he knew Elana's soul, even though he had never met her. He said that he had never said this about anyone else before, but he saw her soul resting with the matriarchs (Sarah, Rivkah, Rachel, and Leah) in the World to Come. Had he said it about almost anyone else, I would probably have laughed. But about Elana — I didn't need to be a Kabbalist to know that he was right.

These few pages cannot truly do justice to the thirty years of life of a very special young woman. I hope that you have at least gained a sense of who Elana was and why she had such a massive impact on all who were fortunate enough to know her. May her soul be bound in the bonds of eternal life.

Where Did We Come From?

Elana and I came from very different backgrounds.

She grew up in Allentown, Pennsylvania, in a home with strong Torah values. Her family is steeped in *chesed* and deeply involved in the community. She loved going to shul from a very early age. She enjoyed learning. She would help others whenever and wherever she could. From the minute she became cognizant of the world, her focus was straight and unswerving: to serve her Creator in the best way possible.

Elana's high school graduation picture.

I lived a very different life.

I grew up in Liverpool, and while my family was strongly Jewish, they lived a much more secular lifestyle. I won't bore you with the nitty-gritty, but at seventeen years of age, I found myself living with a cousin of mine and a black alcoholic friend of his called Ray, and,

Myself at age seventeen.

for a short time, Ray's drinking buddy, Johnny.

The four of us flatmates lived in Lark Lane, a very trendy area of Liverpool, while my parents had moved six thousand miles away to Los Angeles.

The drug that killed Ray in the end was heroin, "smack" as it was referred to — or, if you came from Liverpool, "smach." I often came home from high school to find Ray sprawled on the couch, deep in his drug-induced dreams.

I must say that Ray was good to me. He realized I was a young, unworldly Jewish boy and took it as his personal mission to toughen me up. Many a time, he'd jump on me and see how far he could twist my arm behind my back before I begged for mercy. Looking at it from an outsider's point of view, it might sound a little strange — but there was method in his madness and I always appreciated his "training sessions."

I remember once, when my jacket was stolen from my car in broad daylight, he insisted that we chase after the thieves. We (read: "he") caught them, and I, the little Jewish boy, sat terrified in the car while he "sorted them out."

It was at times like this when I wondered what life was all about and why exactly we were here. But I never took my inquiries any further.

But when I did start searching, I realized I had been given a head start. I had always gone to a Jewish school — by chance much more than design. It was a secular Jewish school and over 50 percent of the student body was non-Jewish (today it is 70 percent), but it had a Jewish identity nevertheless. Jewish studies were mandatory, and when I was sixteen, a rabbi came into my class on the first day of the new term. Surprisingly, he asked a question that to me had nothing whatsoever to do with Judaism. He asked our mixed and mixed-up class who believed in God. As someone who prided himself as a rational scientist (I was hoping one day to become an astronaut) I decidedly did not and was unashamed to say so. "C'mon, Rabbi, these are modern times! Big Bang, evolution, existentialism — get with it, mate," was my general approach.

However, this rabbi was built of different stuff. He was undaunted by our atheism and not ready to be bullied by the intellectual arrogance we represented. He said he could prove to us that there was a God and intended to do so over the next few weeks. He also said that he would prove that this God authored every letter of the Torah.

Well, just his willingness to take on such a tall order earned him some level of respect in our eyes, and we were generally ready to hear what he had to say.

However, after a few classes things changed for me.

He argued his points well and, to my own ears, my responses seemed weak. I tried to tell myself that he was well-rehearsed and expertly trained, but I was shaken. I couldn't pride myself on my scientific approach to life and then go ahead and be dishonest in my approach to God. The bottom line was that this rabbi was making way too much sense for my liking, and I took the only course of action I could to save myself. I refused to attend any more of his classes.

After a good bit of back and forth, and strong discussions with the headmaster, I was given an exemption from Jewish studies — much to the chagrin of the rabbi and much to the envy of my classmates.

That should have been that, but God had other plans.

After about six months of the rabbi's classes, some of my schoolmates started to become religious. I was shocked. These were sophisticated, thinking friends of mine. They weren't the type to run off to a cult and let themselves be brainwashed. But brainwashed they had been, and I felt that I had to take it upon myself to do something about it.

We started having meetings every Tuesday night at which I and another friend met with around four of the "converted" to argue and debate God's existence. I had no interest in the discussion itself; indeed the very topic was distasteful to me. But I felt a responsibility to save my mates from their newfound and eagerly embraced insanity.

We would often talk late into the night, with them eager to suck me in and me eager to suck them out. As you can imagine with such heated discussions, we didn't get all that far.

Life went on and I moved into Lark Lane. My old friends were becoming decidedly Orthodox and I was involved in a rather different lifestyle, which suited me much better. I liked my life and my season ticket to the Saturday soccer games where my team, Liverpool, were the kings of Europe. By April of my senior year, I had already been offered a scholarship to study aeronautical engineering at Caltech in California. That left me five months to coast.

I've met people much further away from Judaism than I was then, but I must say that at this time, I wasn't all that close.

So what happened next was quite a bombshell.

It was April, 1984. A few weeks earlier, the rabbi had invited me for his Pesach seder and I had accepted the invitation with the idea of canceling closer to the time. However, the rabbi didn't let me do that. On the day of the seder, one of his "converts" called me to ask me for a lift. My car had broken down the day before, but where were we going? To a pub, to town? To the rabbi's Pesach seder, was his shocking response. I stuttered and stammered and made excuses, but my fate was sealed. They were expecting me. They had cooked for me. They had set a place for me at the table. They were looking forward to having me. How could I not go?

Any thoughts of making an early getaway were shattered by the time we finally started at 10:00 p.m. I buckled down for the duration.

Myself and a friend putting on tefillin at the Kosel for the first time.

I'd been to family seders in the past and they were always the same. Who cares what Rabbi Eliezer said? What difference does it make if there were fifty or five hundred plagues? And my uncle's personal favorite: We are the ones who are free, so why do we have to eat matzah? Let the Egyptians eat this stuff! The only bit I ever looked forward to was when my two brothers-in-law got drunk on the four cups and danced on the table to the tune of *Chad Gadya.*

So I came that night expecting the usual bore. And boy was I surprised!

The rabbi brought the seder to life for me for the first time ever. Pesach is not about what happened three thousand years ago. It's about who you are today. Personal freedom is something we are all striving for. Is a smoker free? A drug addict? Isn't slavery a very personal experience — and emancipation a potential that lies within us all? These were the type of questions the rabbi posed and answered throughout the Haggadah. Rabbi Eliezer was no longer talking about Egypt, he was talking about me. It was such a radical turnaround that it was mind-blowing. We chatted and argued and debated till four in the morning — and I was ready for more. I was loving every moment of it. Finally, I had found that Judaism actually spoke to me.

The rabbi suggested I stay the night. It was an innocuous enough suggestion, but it burst my bubble. Staying the night meant shul the next morning. Then probably lunch, then another seder. Before I knew it, I'd be his latest success story. I envisioned a picture of myself pinned on his wall with "convert of the month" emblazoned across the top. No way.

However, I had about a five-mile walk home. And the only real way was through a park called Sefton Park. I hadn't been there in a while, and apparently they'd refurbished it. But it was not a place you walked through alone at four o'clock in the morning.

I had a very stark choice. Walk through the park — and risk my body. Stay at the rabbi's — and risk my soul. It was a no-brainer. I apologized profusely, explained that I had promised to call my parents the next day, and got out the door as quickly as possible.

The entrance to Sefton Park looked dark and foreboding. I picked up a stick and thought about all that Ray had taught me. If someone attacked me, they could do almost anything to me and I would still be okay. The walk was terrifying but uneventful. I arrived at the other side safe and sound.

But then a thought hit me that stopped me in my tracks. So obvious and shocking was it that I couldn't continue walking for quite a few minutes.

What was wrong with me? Why was I so afraid? All the rabbi had ever offered me was honesty and truth. He had only said that he would present evidence and allow me to judge for myself. Why on earth was I running away? So terrified, in fact, that I would risk physical injury rather than investigate further. My lucidity flowed. I had confidence in my mind — if he could "prove" to me that God existed, it meant God did. And what was the point in hiding from it? Surely it was better to face the consequences sooner rather than later. And if he could not prove it to me, then I could happily carry on with wherever life took me. It was a win-win situation.

The more I thought about it over the next few days, the more sense it made. I saw the rabbi and my friends with a different attitude. I was open. I was ready to hear the evidence. And hear it I did. It took me a year and a half to be ready to listen, but only a couple of weeks to feel compelled by what I heard.

I was planning to take a year off university and spend the winter in Austria, getting a license to be a ski instructor. But I had nothing to do for the summer. Most of my friends were going to yeshivah in Jerusalem for six weeks. I felt that before I went to Southern California and left whatever Judaism I might have acquired behind, I owed it to myself to do a proper investigation. I had nothing else scheduled. I was impressed by the evidence I had heard. What else was there to do but go to yeshivah with them?

Those six weeks turned into seven years. I never got my ski instructor license — in fact, I went from skiing twice a year for fifteen years to not skiing at all for the next fifteen years. But I have to say that when I finally did get on skis again (on a vacation with my second wife, Chana), it was just like riding a bicycle. You never forget.

I gave up my scholarship at Caltech. Instead, I studied long and hard hours at Aish HaTorah Yeshiva, learned to teach, became a rabbi, and married Elana. I remember saying in my wedding speech that the road to Judaism had been a long one — at times difficult and even discouraging. But had I known from the outset that this was the road one takes to find a girl like Elana, that and that alone would have made it all worthwhile...

Chapter 1

PAIN AND SUFFERING

The book of Job is surely the most shocking book of the Bible.

Job is a righteous man — there is "no one like him on earth; pure, straight, God-fearing, and does no evil" (Job 1:8). He is wealthy, accomplished, respected, and the father of ten children.

God decides to test Job. And it's not a stubbing-one's-toe type of test. In one fell swoop, his children die and his wealth is completely obliterated.

"Naked I left my mother's womb and naked shall I return. God gave and God took back. May the name of God be blessed" (Job 1:21). This is Job's answer. If ever there was a noble and dignified response to suffering, this is surely it. It seems as though Job's faith is unshakable.

Now God ups the stakes and covers Job's entire body with horribly painful blisters. Once again, his response is incredible. His wife asks why he is still blessing God when God has put him through all this, and he says to her, "We have accepted the good from God, shall we not also accept the bad from Him?" (Job 2:10).

His three friends come to visit him and are stunned by what they see has happened. They are left speechless. They sit with Job for seven days without a single word passing between them.

At the end of the seven days, for no apparent reason, Job snaps. A more drastic turnaround could not be imagined. He rants and he raves. He complains and he curses. He says, "Why did I not die in my mother's womb?" and "Never did I feel secure, never quiet, never at peace and now torment?" (ibid. 3:10 and 3:25). Later on, he says, "Even if I were to call and He [God] were to answer me, I don't believe He would listen to my voice. For He has shattered me in a tempest for no good reason" (ibid., 9:16–17). "I am disgusted with my life" (ibid. 9:21). "My days are so few — leave me alone, distance Yourself from me so that I can find some respite. Before I depart, never to return, to a land of gloom and of death's shadow, a land darkened by the darkness of death's shadow and chaos — its brightest spots grim darkness" (ibid. 10:20–22). "His anger slashed me — He hates me" (ibid. 16:9).

I could go on; Job certainly does. Within moments, he has turned from a righteous and holy man, accepting of God's challenges, to an embittered existentialist philosopher.

His friends try to comfort him. And these are no ordinary friends. All are prophets, men of spiritual greatness. Each tries to tell him of God's goodness and ultimate justice. And to each, Job's arguments back are scathing, sarcastic, and bitter. It's hard to believe that we are listening to the same man.

The oral tradition itself seems to struggle with the book of Job. On the question of when he lived, there are no less than fifteen different opinions — more than on any other topic in the Gemara. I once asked my teacher, Rabbi Weinberg, how he understands the message of the book. He said that in his opinion, Job is certainly a good man. He is a righteous man, a man who trusts in God. But the bottom line is that suffering is not easy. It's not easy to lose all your property and not be bothered, to lose all your children and keep smiling. It's not easy to go through terrible pain and continue to bless God. Facing pain is not easy for even the greatest of human beings. Anyone can crack under pressure — as did Job.

To me, this is an incredibly encouraging message. Only God is perfect. We are mere human beings. And when we go through pain — as we all do — it can be overwhelming. We may respond with frustration, bitterness, and even anger and resentment towards God.

And that's okay.

God understands. As much as He does get frustrated, so to speak, with Job (and after thirty-five chapters of ranting and raving, we are all pretty frustrated with Job), at the same time, God still comes to him in the end and His soliloquies are the longest in the Bible, spoken by God directly. God takes the time to comfort Job's troubled heart and in the end turns him around. Job rants and raves, and God takes it from him and then comforts him.

I don't know how to emphasize this point enough. I'm going to write a lot about how to deal with pain, how to have a healthy attitude towards suffering. But throughout it all, this will be my underlying message. We're human. We can hear the most wonderful and uplifting ideas about what pain means and how to grow from it, but pain will still be pain, and sometimes we feel overwhelmed by it. If a man such as Job is allowed to lose it for a little while, then so is any one of us.

I'm not suggesting that we do! It's certainly better to remain strong and steadfast in the face of challenge. However, I'm saying that we're God's children and if suffering makes us angry at Him, He understands that it's not easy.

Moshe

There's a man in Jerusalem who's one of the happiest people I've ever met. With tremendous concentration, he can move his right hand a tiny amount, but apart from that, he is paralyzed from the neck down. I will call him Moshe.

Back in the 60s, Moshe was in his twenties and studying at a college in the U.S. He was good looking, athletic, from a relatively affluent family, and an "A" student. By the standards of his society, he had it all.

Then the race riots began. A black man walked onto his campus looking to shoot a white man; no one in particular, as long as he was white. Moshe was the first man he came across and he shot Moshe in the neck.

Moshe was in a coma for a time, and when he finally came to he was told that he would be paralyzed for the rest of his life.

Moshe says that his first response was, *How could this happen to me?* He thought about this for a long time, and a further question developed.

Now that he did not have the use of his arms or legs, what was it that would make life worth living?

His thoughts flowed further. And when he *had* had the use of his arms and legs, had that made life worth living? What had he been living for up until this point? Had he ever considered what life was about in the first place? It was certainly not about having arms and legs. It's just that when he had arms and legs he had enough distractions not to have to worry about what life was about.

But now that they were useless, he was forced to figure out what he was living for.

More thoughts occurred to him.

If he had not been paralyzed, would he have ever stopped and thought about what he was living for? Almost certainly not. So what is worse, he asked himself — for a person to go through his whole life without the use of his arms and legs; or for a person to go through his whole life with no idea what he is living for? Given the choice, he said to himself, he would take the former.

Eventually Moshe became an Orthodox Jew and moved to Jerusalem. He married a woman who is totally devoted to him and welcomes many guests to his table every Shabbat. During the time I spent there, I found his home full of joy. His disability does not impede his happiness. In fact, in some strange way, it enhances it.

It was always difficult for me to comprehend how someone who is so clearly good should be given such a test. Why did bad things happen to good people like Moshe? Equally, however, it was difficult for me to understand how he could find happiness in the midst of such tragedy.

That was before Elana passed away. Nowadays, the answers to those questions seem obvious to me.

Why Do Bad Things Happen to Good People?

The question is one that Elana and I struggled with over the difficult years of her illness. Eventually, we found an answer that satisfied us both. And its simplicity always amazed me. It needs no drum rolls or introduction. The answer is simply this:

Bad things do not happen to good people.

And bad things don't happen to bad people either. Bad things simply don't "happen." I'm not playing with words. I'm merely using, as I'll explain, the most meaningful definitions available.

The question of why bad things happen is not a new one — it's as old as Judaism itself and is raised in many, many places.

"It is not in our hands — neither the suffering of the righteous nor the comfort of the wicked," says Rabbi Yannai in *Pirkei Avos* 4:15.

How can we possibly understand, in the context of a loving Father in Heaven, people dying young, parents losing children, disease, starvation, wars, gas chambers, and crematoria? It just doesn't seem to work.

But as difficult as it is emotionally, as I have said, I believe it to be quite simple intellectually. And I believe this is exactly what Rabbi Yannai meant when he said, "It is not in our hands." It's like a hot coal. You can see a hot coal from afar; you can understand what it is and why it is; but that does not mean you can pick it up. You can never hope to hold it in your bare hands and feel comfortable with it, only to observe it from a distance.

The same is true when it comes to suffering. If we are able to distance our emotions from the issue, we will be able to deal with it and understand it relatively easily. Like the hot coal, from afar, it can be observed and understood.

But we can never touch.

We feel suffering deeply — be it our own or that of others. We cannot merely stand back and give answers. As much as we might understand it intellectually, we will nevertheless never feel happy with any answer that we give ourselves. Answers will always seem callous in the face of human pain. We cannot merely "explain" to someone why their child died. The pain is tangible and the explanation is theoretical. The person is suffering, experiencing real pain, and we are merely parroting words. Answers don't solve the problem. They don't take away the horror. They don't soothe; they irritate. We can understand them, but never find complete comfort in them.

However, just because we might not feel comfortable with answers does not mean that they are wrong. When Elana found the lump, it was cancer. We did not like the fact that it was cancer, but that did not change the reality.

The answer to suffering is the same. It is not a pleasant answer, but a person who wants truth above pleasantries will see that it is correct.

I ask you, the reader, to put aside emotion as best you can and to try to listen with your head and not your heart. To the extent to which you are able to do so is the extent to which you will find meaningful answers in the following chapters.

Why?

As a start to this — and most questions in life — we need first to define our terms. And, most significantly, in dealing with why bad happens in this world, we need to begin with a definition of "bad."

I believe that much of our difficulty in dealing with bad things happening comes from a definition of bad that is entirely inconsistent with Judaism.

I would imagine that for most people, the working definition of "bad" is "pain." Bad and pain are basically synonymous. Be it the pain someone goes through while dying from a horrible disease, the pain of someone like Elana, knowing she will never dance at her children's weddings, or the pain of children starving in Africa or the Warsaw Ghetto. It's the pain involved in these situations that makes them "bad." If no one in the Holocaust went through any pain — if they were gently put to sleep without any knowledge of what was happening — it would still be a horrible thing, but it would not bother us in the way that it does. Take a few moments to consider this, because it's important to understand exactly what it is that bothers us before moving on.

If pain is to be in any way linked with our definition of bad — be it emotional, physical, or spiritual pain — then the question of why bad things happen to people is fairly well unanswerable. Because pain happens to every human being, righteous or evil, throughout most of their lives. And if pain in and of itself is bad, then God has clearly made a world that is just filled with "bad."

Let's re-examine our assumptions for a moment. Is all pain necessarily bad? Defining pain as "bad" is actually a modern phenomenon. Let me give just a few very obvious illustrations as to why we cannot view all pain as automatically being bad.

Daniel

I once had a guest, Daniel, over for dinner. He was in the process of recovering from a coma that he had been in for two years, due to massive brain hemorrhaging during an operation. He had still not regained his sense of touch and so could not feel anything anywhere in his body.

As a little boy, I had heard about people like Daniel, who have no sense of touch. And I was incredibly jealous. If only it happened to me, I used to think, I would never feel pain again in my life — no painful injections, no dentist's drill, no pain when I fall off my bike. If only I could have no sense of touch, life would be wonderful. It was only as an adult that I realized how disastrous this would actually be and it was brought home to me very clearly when Daniel came for dinner.

I had noticed that he had been nervous about eating during dinner, but it was only when I gave him a cup of tea for dessert that I realized why. He asked one of our children to test it for him and see how hot it was. Without being able to feel, he was unable to judge temperature and he could very easily drink boiling hot tea, and scald his mouth and throat, without even realizing that he was doing so. With his early warning system of pain gone, he could be destroying his body without noticing. Were he to tread on a piece of glass, for example, he could continue walking without knowing that he was tearing his foot to shreds. Yes, he felt no pain, but because of that, he could not even drink a cup of tea without someone else's help.

Physical pain is clearly something very beneficial and necessary for us.

Cancer is another obvious example. A lack of pain in its early stages is one of the main reasons why it is such a deadly disease. Were cancer to be painful immediately, very few people would actually die from it. If cancer could be felt the moment it began, doctors could respond to it at a very early stage. They could cut it out before it had a chance to spread to other parts of the body. Unfortunately, this is not the case. Rarely is the disease detected by a person feeling pain. Our doctor told us that Elana's cancer had certainly existed for months, and possibly even years, before she detected it. Cancer is deadly precisely because it begins painlessly.

In the case of cancer, as with Daniel, it is the lack of pain that is the "bad" thing — and a very "bad" thing at that. Pain would actually be a "good thing" in these circumstances.

Clearly, pain is a complex phenomenon. To merely label it as "bad" is to oversimplify the matter.

A Broken Leg

To take this a little further, let's imagine that someone is walking down the street, minding his own business — maybe even on the way to do a good deed! — and a car, driven by someone who is drunk, mounts the curb and runs him over. His leg is broken in four places and he requires an immediate operation, with six weeks recovery in the hospital afterwards.

Good or bad?

Obviously it's bad, you say. And why did such a "bad" thing happen to a person who was on his way to do a good deed?

Yet, if we jump so quickly to this conclusion, we are again making the mistake of oversimplification.

Let's say the operation goes well and our patient is recuperating in a hospital ward. The next day, he meets a young lady in the same ward. She is also going to be in the hospital for a few weeks. They start talking. They don't get on so well at first, but as time goes by they begin to like each other. After all, if you talk to someone for hours each day, you will eventually find something you like about them. Their attraction grows over time. They find that they have many shared interests. They are from similar backgrounds and have the same life goals. Once out of the hospital, they start going out. After a short while, they become engaged. Eventually, they marry and live happily ever after.

Now, let's ask this man, fifty years later, as he sits with his great-grandchildren on his lap at his golden wedding anniversary, whether it was a good or bad thing that the car ran him over on that fateful day. Looking back, he would in no way consider it a bad thing. Painful, yes, but it was pain that brought an incredible amount of goodness in its wake. If you were to offer him the opportunity to go back in time and not be hit by that car, he would not dream of taking it.

This is an example of short term pain that brings long term results. The pain of his broken leg disappeared after a few weeks. The goodness of his marriage to the woman he met in the hospital was eternal.

Pain is not always "bad."

And when I talk about pain, I don't just mean physical pain. I'm just using it as the simplest illustration. The exact same points could be made and similar examples brought for emotional pain such as fear, terror, sadness, loss, and abuse.

In my situation, as a very simple example, the pain I went through — the loss, the sadness, the fear, the loneliness — in losing Elana has made me infinitely more capable of reaching out and comforting others who experience loss.

Defining "Bad"

I hope that by now it's obvious that "pain" is not useful as a definition for "bad." Perhaps some pain really is bad (though we as yet have no examples of that type of pain), but certainly not all pain is bad. And so we are going to have to refine our definition.

At this point, we might be tempted to redefine bad as "pain that brings no positive results." But then it would be impossible for us to ever decide whether something was good or bad. For who is to say what good might come in ten years or twenty, or perhaps not even in this world, but in the next one? Such a definition of "bad" would be of no use to us whatsoever. Until we were fully aware of the ramifications of any event — in both this world and the next — we could not make a judgment that it was "bad" (or "good" for that matter). To define "bad" in this way would be tantamount to having no definition of "bad" whatsoever.

Because of this, the best we can say is: Pain, in and of itself, is fairly neutral. It's not pleasant, it's not comfortable, it's not nice, but it's also neither bad nor good.

Why God might make something painful or create the entire concept of pain in the first place are issues that I will deal with at a later stage, but pain has no meaningful role in trying to define "bad."

The Jewish Definition

We Jews have a very different definition of bad — and based on this definition, nothing bad ever really "happens" in this world.

"Good" is something that enables you to become more Godly. And conversely, "bad" is something that makes you a less Godly person. Torah is good. Mitzvos are good. God Himself is good. Moving away from God — the source and root of all goodness — is bad.

Put a different way, good is that which leads us towards self-perfection, that which enables us to become the great human beings we are capable of becoming, that which helps us to find the closeness to God that is available to us. Bad is that which takes us away from God, that which hinders us from achieving our potential.

These are the Jewish definitions and the ones I will generally use for the rest of this book. It's worth taking just a few minutes to consider the implications of these definitions before reading any further.

Let's take a look at pain in the context of these definitions.

As a rule, does pain and difficulty in life make it easier or harder to rise spiritually? If we are honest, we would have to say that challenge helps us towards greatness. Greatness is not usually found among those who spend their days lying on beaches and sailing around the world in million-dollar yachts. Greatness is much more often found among those who face adversity head on and overcome it. Those who achieve their true potential are those who struggle through difficult situations and build their character in the process. The Gemara tells us, "Be careful of the children of the poor, for from them Torah comes" (*Nedarim* 81a).

Far from being a hindrance, hardship is actually something that assists us in this world. If "good" is something that can help us come closer to God, then hardship is certainly "good."

Let's revisit the man with the broken leg — even without knowing that he ended up meeting his future wife due to it. Let's look at it as a plain and simple broken leg; seemingly nothing more gained other than pain and temporary disability. Is that good or bad?

The Jewish answer is still, of course, neither. But now there is something to add.

It could be good, or it could be bad. It all depends on what this man does with it. A broken leg can make him angry and upset and take him away from God. Or it can push him to evaluate where he can mend his ways and bring himself closer to God.

The choice is entirely his.

The broken leg is certainly a challenge — but if our friend rises to the challenge and overcomes it, he will lift himself to a more Godly realm. It is not good or bad. It is, however, a significant opportunity for good — should he choose for it to be so. And if he does, then he will look back fifty years later and say that yes, it was wonderful that he met his wife through his broken leg, but even more wonderfully, the broken leg enabled him to employ his free will to lift himself to new levels of personal greatness.

There is nothing — absolutely nothing — that happens to us in this world that is good or bad. It is all completely neutral. But everything that happens does have the potential to lift us to a greater level of goodness — or drag us further away from God. Everything has the potential to be good and everything has the potential to be bad. "Bad" things don't happen to good people. But neither do "good" things. Things happen that are either more or less painful. But they are not inherently good or bad. We human beings are the sole arbiters as to whether that which occurs in our lives will ultimately be good or bad. The choice is entirely within our hands.

Elana and I made a decision when she first became ill. We didn't have a choice as to whether or not she would have cancer. But we did have a choice as to how we would respond to that cancer. We knew that we could allow ourselves to despair, that we could hide ourselves away from the world and accept our "fate." Or we could decide to be happy with the goodness that we had. We could make sure we enjoyed our time with each other and our children and enjoyed our lives in general. We knew that we could grow closer to God at this time or we could move further away — and that choice was entirely within our hands.

The Mishnah tells us that Abraham was tested with ten tests — to show how much God loved him (*Pirkei Avos* 5:3). At first glance this seems strange. Here's how you show you love someone? Firstly, you have him thrown into a furnace. Then, you tell him to pack his bags and move to a foreign country. When he obeys, you bring a famine to this country. And then, when he travels to find food, you have the ruler of the next place abduct his wife. He gets her back and returns to his ordained place of residence, only to find that his nephew has been kidnapped by four powerful kings. He manages to release him and is then commanded to kill his only son. Upon his return, having overcome the greatest challenge of his life, he finds that his wife has died and he is forced to pay an exorbitant sum for an inferior burial plot in a land that God has supposedly promised him as an inheritance. And all of this shows God's love for Abraham?!

Yes! This is precisely God's love. Because through these challenges, Abraham was able to come closer to God. He fulfilled his potential and became the great human being we know of, founder of the nation that has taught monotheism to most of the world. The pain was short-lived. The results were eternal. Abraham sits in his place in eternity, not in spite of his pain, but because of it.

His pain is gone. His greatness remains forever.

And so, I ask you to ask yourself, and to be brutally honest — what are you in this world for? To be comfortable? To avoid pain? To live out seventy or eighty years of life with the least challenge possible? If this is your aim, then many "bad" things will happen along the way — because this is a world of pain and pain is antithetical to all that you are living for. If, however, you believe, as I do, that we are here to lift ourselves into Godliness, to grow and to ultimately attain self-perfection, then all that happens to us is a golden opportunity — and the more challenging it is, the greater that opportunity. The Mishnah tells us that "according to the pain is the reward" (*Pirkei Avos* 5:23). It doesn't say "effort," it says "pain." The level of pain defines the level of potential for Godliness. Of course, we don't go looking for pain, but when it comes, we embrace it as an opportunity to strive towards perfection.

The Rabbis take this to its logical extreme. They say that if someone has had nothing painful happen to him for forty days, he should worry greatly (*Eiruvin* 16b). They say that perhaps he has "acquired his world." This means that God is no longer testing him, no longer giving him the opportunity to grow. God has given up on him ever becoming anything more than he is right now and has simply chosen to let him live out his days in this world without attaining deeper levels of perfection. A life free from difficulty is not something that interests us as Jews. Painful as they may be, we do actually want the challenges that will help us achieve our potential.

At the height of Elana's illness, and at the times of my deepest pain afterwards, this is what I kept reminding myself. I put signs up all around my house saying, "We are in this world to use our free will to get closer to God — nothing else." We all have different scenarios in which we are placed — some more painful, some less. But it is all directed towards the same end. Specific circumstances merely give us a context in which to use our free will to lift ourselves towards Godliness. Borrowing from Shakespeare, I would think of every human being as acting in a giant play — a play that lasts seventy or so years — and a play in which there will be great drama and tragedy. Each has a different script, a different challenge. The acts and scenes may be different, but the underlying plot is the same for all six billion of us. We are charged with the mission of using our free will and lifting ourselves closer to God. Circumstances may be fluid, but challenge is a constant — the purpose behind all events in life.

My friends, take it from me, pain passes. All pain passes. If not in this world, then certainly in the next. A cut finger might take a few minutes, a headache an hour, a stomachache a day, a sprained ankle a week, a broken leg a month, and a broken heart may even take a lifetime. But no pain will carry through to the World of Truth. It is the decisions we make, the way we choose to face that challenge and overcome that pain, which will remain with us for eternity. These decisions, and these decisions alone, are the purpose of our years in this world.

Rav Zusha

The story is told of some chassidim who went to their Rebbe to ask why bad things happen to good people. His response was simple: "Why ask me? Nothing bad has ever happened to me."

He felt unqualified to answer the question, as it was purely theoretical for him. Life had been good to him and nothing bad had ever really happened to him. The person they needed to talk to was Rav Zusha. He could talk to them from personal experience. He had been through real pain in his life. He was so poor that he could not even afford a pair of shoes. He had suffered great illness. He had lost close family members. You name it, it had happened to Rav Zusha.

The chassidim traveled a long way to find Rav Zusha and confronted him with the same question. Why did bad things happen to good people? His response was simple:

"Why ask me? Nothing bad has ever happened to me."

He felt unqualified to answer the question, as it was purely theoretical for him. Life had been good to him and nothing bad had ever really happened to him. Painful, yes. Difficult, yes. But bad? No way.

He was not putting on a show for them; he meant every word he said. Everything he had been through had brought him closer to God. From his perspective, his life was filled with true goodness. Poverty had brought him closer to God. Illness had brought him closer to God. Losing those he loved had brought him closer to God. So where was the bad? He certainly didn't perceive it. There was pain, but much of it had passed and that which had not yet passed would also pass. He had faced his challenges and achieved greatness through them.

Rav Zusha's response brought him closer to God. Some would have responded in the same way. Yet others would have chosen to distance themselves from their Creator. It is all up to us; it is our choice.

The Holocaust

This idea of the supremacy of personal choice is true even in the most extreme of circumstances. I have met many survivors of the Holocaust, all of whom were put through the most horrific experiences. There are those whose response was to turn away from God, but for some, it brought them even closer. It is a common myth to believe that the Holocaust pushed all those who experienced it away from God. Those who did distance themselves from God are perhaps more vociferous, but there are many others who responded very differently.

Before I go further, let me state that it is not for us, who did not go through such horrors, to judge those who did. We did not experience their pain and terror and are in no position to question why they did what they did. But one thing is clear. While the experience itself was not in their hands, their response to it was. Some chose to turn away from God; some chose to find solace and renewed faith in God. For those who turned away from God, it was their free choice that caused them to do so, not the Holocaust. To be sure, the Holocaust was a catalyst. But for many, also, the Holocaust was a catalyst for coming closer to their Creator. That was their choice also.

None of us can possibly know how we would have responded in those most horrific of circumstances and, as I have already said, it is not for us to pass judgment. But one thing is for sure — whatever might be denied us in this world, the ability to choose to grow from our experiences or to become resentful can never be taken away from us. We are all complete masters of our own spiritual destiny.

One of my most significant insights into this aspect of the Holocaust came in Krakow's old Jewish cemetery. I had brought a group of young Jews to Poland to gain a deeper understanding of the Holocaust, and we were accompanied by a survivor. As Holocaust experiences go, his had been pretty "bad." He was a member of the Sonderkommando in Birkenau. For eleven months, in 1944, he had worked in Crematoria II, taking the still warm bodies of Hungarian Jewry from the gas chambers and putting them in the ovens. He was a direct eyewitness to the murder of hundreds of thousands of Jews. Day after day, for eleven months, he saw the door of a gas chamber close on two thousand living, breathing human beings and saw it open, fifteen minutes later, to a twisted mass of lifeless flesh.

Our group asked him how he felt about God and he said that his belief in God had died in Birkenau. There could be no God after what he had seen.

On our way back from Auschwitz with him, we were visiting the old Jewish cemetery in Krakow and we bumped into another survivor who happened to be an Orthodox Jew. He had been in the Lodz Ghetto and eight different camps, including Auschwitz. He had now brought his two sons from Australia to see where he had grown up. Members of our group were bold enough to ask the question that was on all of our minds — mine included. How could he be an Orthodox Jew after all he had gone through?

We were shocked by the ferocity of the answer he shot back. How could someone not believe in God after the Holocaust? Anyone who survived had to have experienced miracles. In fact, the Holocaust itself was completely supernatural — that the Germans should wish to utterly eliminate a sector of the population that posed no threat to them whatsoever. It made no sense at all without putting God in the picture, was his response.

Not only that, he said, but he would challenge any survivor who did not believe in God on these issues. He said that a survivor might be angry at God. He might want nothing to do with God. He might even hate God. But he could not possibly believe that there was no God.

We mentioned what the survivor who was with our group had said to us and he asked to meet him. Nervously, I introduced them. I don't remember exactly what words passed between them, or how they were said. I just remember that it was passionate and powerful, and for twenty minutes the group stood transfixed listening to the debate. By the end of it all, the survivor who was with us admitted that he did believe in God, but after what he had been through, he did not want to deal with Him anymore. They cried, they embraced, and the other survivor said that he understood.

The second survivor told me he could argue the same point with any other survivor. That's a bold statement. Maybe he can and maybe he can't, but one thing is for sure. The Holocaust, as with all tragedy, has aspects that can move one away from God. But it equally has aspects that can move one closer. What actually happens is entirely within our human hands.

Suffering

At this point, I want to draw an important distinction based on what I have been talking about — the difference between pain and suffering. I have been using the words loosely until now, but they are in actuality subtly, yet very significantly, different.

We all go through pain in this world. It comes at us from the outside. Suffering, however, is self-inflicted. It depends entirely on how we decide to respond to our pain. If we allow pain to take over, to overwhelm us; if we allow ourselves to slip into the attractive comfort of despair, then we suffer. If we face pain and rise to the challenge, then we will still go through the pain, but we do not have to suffer.

Day after day, month after month, year after year, I watched Elana in pain — if not physical, then emotional. She desperately wanted to see her children grow up; she wanted to dance at their weddings, but knew in her heart of hearts that she never would. She went through immense anguish.

Never once, however, did I see her suffer. Not a single moment. Pain was not her enemy. It was her means for growth. Apathy was her enemy. Anger was her enemy. Despair was her enemy. Giving up was her enemy. But not pain.

We can see the same thing in less extreme cases. When a woman gives birth, she goes through tremendous pain, but does she suffer? Bringing up children is incredibly painful — on many levels. But do we call it suffering? Running a marathon is overwhelmingly painful for the last few miles (and if you are as unfit as I am, then for all the miles previous to that also!), but is it suffering?

I think the distinction between pain and suffering is as follows: If we are able to find meaning in pain, then we do not suffer. If we are unable to find meaning in pain, then it becomes overwhelming and we call that feeling of being overwhelmed "suffering."

The simple ability to put pain into a meaningful context enables us to cope with it. Elana used to quote Nietzche saying, "A man can deal with any what, as long as he has a good enough why."

A child, for example, cuts his finger and screams the house down. An adult cuts his finger and gets on with life. Children live in the here and now, so a child has no context for his pain. There is no meaningful future to look forward to, just the immediacy of the pain. An adult realizes that the pain will pass and life will be good again in spite it. He doesn't suffer. And, by the way, why is it that when you hug and kiss a child the pain seems to go? It's not the pain that goes, it's the suffering. You have given the child a meaningful context for the pain — the context of a parent's love. The child still feels the pain, but with a newfound context for it, he no longer suffers.

An adult must find his own meaning in his pain. Sometimes it is obvious, as in the case of a woman in labor. Sometimes it is a little harder. But when he or she can look at the pain as a means to grow, a means to develop deeper self-understanding, then the pain remains, but the suffering will be forgotten.

Everyone goes through pain in life. But not one of us has to suffer if we do not want to. Again, the choice is ours.

Conclusion

As I said at the beginning, bad things do not happen to anyone.

Pain certainly happens. And it doesn't distinguish between good and bad people. (I only mean "good" and "bad" people in terms of perception. In reality, who is any one of us to judge who is good and who is bad? But when people ask the question — why do bad things happen to "good" people — they are referring to "people we perceive as good or bad." So I am using that definition as reference for this point, even though I do not agree with it.) Sometimes a lot of pain happens to people. Sometimes tragic and horrific pain happens to people — good people included. But good people generally, by definition, do not allow that pain to become suffering nor to lead them away from God. Good people will usually choose to find the good in their pain — as they do in all of life.

Sometimes good people, as well as bad, find their pain overwhelming and cannot respond in a positive way. A healthy response to pain is not indicative of a good or bad person; it is just a sign of whether the person will grow closer to God or not as a result of this specific experience.

The point remains the same — circumstances are neutral. We and we alone, make the choice of whether they are to be good or bad.

Chapter 2

Why a World of Pain?

Assuming that one can accept all that I have said so far, it still leaves us with a question. Yes, maybe pain does help us grow and develop. Maybe it is not a "bad" thing after all. But that doesn't take away from the fact that it is still a painful thing. It might not be "bad," but whichever way you look at it, it is "unpleasant." Why couldn't God have simply created a world in which we could grow without any pain at all?

The answer lies in understanding the nature of God.

When Moses stands at the burning bush, he asks God what he should tell the Jewish people. Who should he say is sending him to free them from Egypt? God's answer is seemingly enigmatic: "I will be what I will be" (Exodus 3:14). He tells Moses to tell the Jewish people, " 'I will be' has sent you." Even my Microsoft grammar-checker doesn't like that one, but Moses seems quite satisfied with the answer. He somehow understands this phrase as a deep insight into the essence of God. Allow me to explain what I believe the Torah is telling us.

Everything in creation is defined by and influenced by external forces. An animal is firstly defined by its own particular DNA. Once created, it is now shaped by its environment — its mother, its experiences, its needs and lackings. A lion brought up in a zoo will be a very different lion than one allowed to roam free in the jungle — even if they have identical DNA.

Human beings also have this nature versus nurture business, but we have an added dimension — that of free will. We are firstly influenced by the external forces in our makeup — the nature of our genes — both physical and spiritual. Once we come into the world, there is nurture and experience. But there is also free will — the ability to choose and shape our own destiny. You will often hear of the "nurture/nature" debate — which of the two factors is more significant in human development. We Jews agree with neither side. What truly has the potential to shape us is our free will, who we decide we want to be. And if we do not decide to exercise our own free will, then it is a mixture of both nurture and nature that will define our path in life.

God, however, is completely different from anything in this world. He is "One" — completely unique and incomparable to any aspect of His creation. There is no external force that can shape him, for He is the creator of all forces. There is no existence external to Him. There are no genes that dictated His form. He is defined by one thing and one thing alone — what He is. His essence defines Him. He is not subjected to the limitation of the whims of free will — even His own. This is not a limitation of free will; quite the opposite, it is free will in its perfect form. He is what He is and "will be what He will be." His essence defines Him as perfect, so He cannot make a "decision" to be imperfect. And that essence can never change.

Now we can take a look at creation and see why pain is an unavoidable element. God, the infinite being, created a universe as a natural consequence of His existence. It was a higher level of choice — based not on "personal decision," but rather on absolute reality. Perfection means giving, and giving requires a recipient. So, in effect, God "needs" a universe to which He can give.

However, there is only one thing that God can give and that is Himself. He is, after all, all that exists.

The goodness that He gives, therefore, is the experience of the infinite, of reality, of Him. And herein lies the paradox. God wants to create beings with whom He can have a relationship, but if they are to be takers, then they will be His complete opposite — He will be the absolute giver; His creations, the absolute takers. How then can a relationship exist? Relationships are built upon commonality. If we were to be complete takers, we would have nothing in common with God.

As a result, He had to create a mechanism in which the beings He created would "earn" their intimacy with Him. They would struggle to be like Him and, in so doing, they would come close to Him. This is why God created the concept of free will. The only way for God to be able to give in a meaningful way is for Him to create beings who can choose for themselves. They can choose whether or not to be Godly.

And for free will to be at all meaningful, it must be real. There must be very real opportunities to move away from Godliness. If it is all a sham, then it serves no purpose. We need real decisions with real consequences.

So God, in His infinite wisdom, created two stages to our existence. First is a stage when we can use our free will to "earn" our relationship with Him. And second is a stage in which we can enjoy the closeness to God which we have earned. This is the reason for this world and the next.

But why would a being that God created choose to move away from Godliness? In a Godly world, why would it want anything else?

Here is where the concept of pain comes in.

Pain is what creates the choice. The fact that we are beings who hate pain, who look to avoid pain and effort at all costs, means that we can have free will. Yes, we are pulled to Godliness, but what if there is pain to be overcome in order to get there? What if the world is one of "no pain, no gain"? Now a balance can be created and we must choose between the difficult and often painful path of coming closer to God or the easy and more comfortable path of drifting away. Without pain, free will would be utterly meaningless. There would be no challenge and hence we would be unable to "earn" our relationship with God.

Even free-will decisions that are between desire and control of desire are essentially still pain based. It's an effort and a struggle to control a desire. It's much more comfortable to allow it to express itself. As someone who has dieted frequently, I know that holding back from eating chocolate cake when on a diet is a "painful" experience.

We are placed in this world to be tested and challenged — and in so doing, we "earn" our "reward" in eternity. Pain enables us to be challenged by the world and thus actualize our potential of coming closer to God. This world is a series of tests over which to triumph, so that we can gradually become greater and greater human beings.

With this in mind, it also makes sense that the closer one gets to God, the greater the trials must be. If a person has overcome an easy test, thus actualizing a certain amount of potential, then the next stage must be more difficult. Those who face increasingly challenging circumstances should be the "good" people — because they are the ones who will benefit most.

The greatest reward a good person could want for overcoming a difficult and painful challenge is an even harder challenge — an opportunity to come even closer to God. I mentioned earlier that Abraham was tested with ten tests — to show how much he was beloved before God. Each of these tests was more challenging than the one before, until he reached the pinnacle of his life: willing to kill his only son because God commanded him to do so.

We Jews do not ask for challenges. Who is arrogant enough to believe he will be victorious? Yet, when they come, we relish our challenges, for they are the true opportunities of life.

If we define bad as something painful, then contrary to what we might initially have expected, "bad" will probably happen to good people more often than to anyone else.

Corrective Pain

Challenging us to greatness is the primary purpose of pain, but there is also a secondary purpose.

As I said earlier, in order for free will not to be a sham, the option to choose to move away from God must be a real one. We must be able to drift away and then away again and then still further.

Let's say one of God's created beings does this. Now God has three choices, none of which are all that appealing:

1. God can take away the person's free will and bring him back by force — hence rendering his existence utterly meaningless. He would do this person a greater service by simply removing him from the world.

2. God can do nothing and allow the person to continue his course of action. This would make the person's existence worse than meaningless. Not only would he not be accomplishing God's purpose in his being created, but he would actually be moving farther and farther away from it and creating much destruction in his wake.
3. God can give some sort of subtle message that would not interfere with free will, but would make the person wake up and see that this is not a healthy course of action.

These three choices are the same ones parents have with their children. Take, for example, a child who is becoming involved in drugs. His parents have a number of choices:

1. They can lock him in his room forever — thus solving the problem, but making his life meaningless. He may be unable to take anymore drugs, but he cannot do anything else in life either.
2. They can take no action and allow him to continue doing drugs — risking that he will destroy himself. This would probably be the most callous of all decisions a parent can make.
3. They can create natural consequences to his actions, so that there is pain commensurate to his mistakes — not so much pain that it takes away his free choice, but enough to help him realize that perhaps this is not how he wants to live. They could threaten to cut off money or other benefits he has been enjoying — perhaps even throw him out of the house.

In drug counseling, the only time at which most addicts start on the process of rehabilitation is when they have reached rock bottom; when they are penniless, on the streets, with no friends and no one to help them. At that point, they just might realize that drugs are destroying their life and be ready for change. Only the pain of their situation is strong enough to shake them out of their apathy.

Difficult as it might be for parents, creating painful consequences is often the only way to deal with children in distress. It is often also the only way that God can help His children, here in this world.

When we make mistakes, He creates consequences so that we may wake up to the fact that this is not how we want to be living. We might wake up, but then again, we might not. Free will remains a constant. There is a message, but it is only effective if we respond in the correct way. The consequences are not strong enough to compel us to change; they are merely there to gently coax us in the right direction. The choice, as always, is our own.

Pain and hardship are often (though not always) God's means of waking us up to mistakes we are making. This is not "punishment." It is a wake-up call for us to rediscover our purpose in life.

The Rabbis tell us that when a person sees troubles coming upon him, he should examine his deeds (*Berachos* 5a). Pain, in addition to being a crucial cog in the mechanism for free will, is also used to convey a message. It is not a punishment. It is there to tell us that we are doing something wrong — to show us that we need to adjust our mode of action.

And pain is not really a direct response to our actions. Judaism looks at it more as cause and effect.

Just as there is physical cause and effect, so too is there spiritual cause and effect. We don't say that if you jump off a building, God will punish you by pulverizing you to death. We say that if you jump off a building, your body will be pulverized as a direct consequence of hitting the hard ground at great velocity. Similarly, we say that if you jump off a spiritual building, there will be consequences — not punishments — consequences.

Pain, therefore, serves two purposes.

First, it creates a challenge through which we can choose to come closer to God. This is what the Mishnah says, "God tested Abraham with ten tests, to show how great was His love for Abraham."

And second, it is used as a mechanism for waking us up to our mistakes.

There is a third purpose for pain found in Rabbinic writing, which is the concept of *kapparah*, atonement. I don't want to go deeply into this topic, but in simple terms it is a more sophisticated extension of the second aspect of pain. God does not bring pain to "cleanse" us of our transgressions. *Kapparah* enables a person who has already changed his direction in the necessary way, to find the deepest levels of oneness within that change.

An example might be that of a person who overindulges in food. He then comes to an intellectual realization that this is wrong and as a result goes through a process of self-correction. However, it's all a little cerebral, and staying up all night with a stomachache will make his understanding of his own stupidity much more real and deeply ingrained. God might do this for him in order that he can internalize his regret more deeply and feel a commitment to being different more strongly.

A wealthy man who turned his back on poor people but has now realized his mistake and become very generous might still not feel deeply enough for the change to be complete until he has been lost in a desert for a week with no food or drink and with no one to reach out to him.

You might assume from this that those making the most mistakes in life should go through the most pain.

But there is another factor to take into account.

Let's say you have two children. One does well in school. He is a loving, caring, diligent child. He has a good crowd of friends and spends his spare time visiting his grandparents or furthering his quest for wisdom. He excels at all that he does and is loved by all.

Your other child, however, is the type who just can't seem to get his life in order. He's a failure in school. He's in with the wrong crowd. He's rude and abusive to his parents and others around him and never does anything for anyone other than himself.

One day, you hear that your two children have been out shoplifting together. You cannot believe it, but the facts are undeniable. With which one would you be more upset?

It's obvious that you would be more upset with the "good" child, with the child who usually gets things right. From the child who is struggling, you'd expect such a thing. But from the child who is doing so well — to steal?! He has set his standards so high that your expectations are also high, and therefore, your anger and frustration are much greater.

The same is true of God and His children. The Sages tell us that God judges the righteous "to a hair's breadth" (*Yevamos* 121a). Those who come close to him are held much more accountable for their actions than those who are distant. God expects more from them because they expect more from themselves.

Why would God be hard on someone who won't change anyway? It makes more sense to come down hard on the one who just might get the point.

As I mentioned earlier, the Sages make a remarkable statement: "A person who has had nothing painful happen to him in forty days has 'acquired his world.'"

How is it possible for a human being to go for forty days without either a challenge or a wake-up call? Why has God put him or her in this world if not to grow? It cannot be that this person is completely righteous, for in such a case, while he would perhaps need no wake-up calls, his challenges would nevertheless increase. God constantly pushes the righteous to grow more, achieve more, develop more — to help lift them to greater levels of Godliness.

The only possible scenario for an effortless forty-day period is as follows: A person becomes so distant from God that challenges will only push him further away and wake-up calls will achieve nothing. Such a person will be unable to experience God in a future existence. But for the few good choices he must have made during his lifetime, God is able to give him some level of goodness in this world. It's not a punishment to grant him goodness in this world, as opposed to in the next. As one so completely tied to this world, it's the only place in which he will be able to appreciate any goodness that is bestowed. Therefore, such a person will receive a life of goodness, with no challenges and no setbacks for the period of time his amount of goodness has earned him. He will be given his "next world" in this one — hence the phrase "acquired his world." Forty days without any trouble whatsoever is a very clear sign that a person is in such a situation.

Problems, in Judaism, far from being something bad, are a sign of spiritual vigor and vibrancy.

The more a person moves forward, the more he or she will be faced with challenge and difficulty.

This may not sound like much of an incentive to grow spiritually, but that is only if you look at pain as a "bad" thing. As I have said before and will say again — pain is not our enemy; distance from God is our enemy. Pain is the means through which we can fight the enemy and win the battle of this world. We can learn not to be frustrated and upset by pain, but rather to embrace it as a friend which is here to help us fulfill our potential. Then we will have the ability to deal with the question of "bad" things happening.

The China Teacup

I read a story once that illustrates this point.

> A couple once took an anniversary trip to England and were shopping in a shop of beautiful things.
>
> They both liked antiques and pottery, and especially teacups. Spotting an exceptional cup, the woman said, "May we see that? It's so beautiful..."
>
> As the lady handed the teacup to them, suddenly it began to speak, "You don't understand. I have not always been a teacup. There was a time when I was just a lump of red clay.
>
> "My master took me and rolled me and pounded and me, over and over, and I yelled out, 'Don't do that. I don't like it! Let me alone!' But he only smiled, and said, 'Not yet...'
>
> "Then, WHAM! I was placed on a spinning wheel and spun around and around.
>
> " 'Stop it! I'm getting dizzy! I'm going to be sick!' I screamed.
>
> "But the master only nodded and said quietly, 'Not yet.'
>
> "He spun me and poked and prodded and bent me out of shape to suit himself and then...then he put me in an oven. I had never felt such heat. I yelled and knocked and pounded at the door. 'Help! Get me out of here!'
>
> "I could see him through the glass door and I could read his lips as he shook his head from side to side, 'Not yet.'
>
> "When I thought I couldn't bear it another minute, he opened the door, carefully took me out, and put me on a shelf, where I began to cool. Oh, that felt so good! 'This is much better,' I thought. But, after I cooled off, he picked me up and brushed me and painted me all over. The fumes were horrible. I thought I would gag. 'Oh, please! Stop it, stop it!'

I cried. He only shook his head and said. 'Not yet.'

"Then, suddenly, he put me back in the oven. Only it was not like the first one. This oven was twice as hot, and I just knew I would suffocate. I begged. I pleaded. I screamed. I cried. I was convinced I would never make it. I was ready to give up.

"Just then the door opened and he took me out and again placed me on the shelf, where I cooled off and waited, wondering, 'What's coming next?'

"Then he handed me a mirror and said, 'Look at yourself.' And I did. 'That's not me!' I said. 'That couldn't be me. It's beautiful...I'm beautiful!'

"And then he spoke: 'I know it hurt to be rolled and pounded and patted, but had I left you alone, you would have dried up. I know it made you dizzy to spin around on the wheel, but if I had stopped, you would have crumbled. I know it was hot and you suffered terribly in the oven, but if I hadn't put you there, you would have cracked. I know the fumes were bad when I painted you, but if I hadn't done that, you never would have hardened. You never would have had any color in your life. And if I hadn't put you in that second oven, you wouldn't have survived for long, because your hardness would not have held.

" 'Now you are a finished product. Now you are what I had in mind when I first began with you.' "

God is the potter, and we are His clay. He will mold us and make us, and expose us to just enough pressures of just the right kinds that we may become a flawless piece of work to fulfill His good, pleasing, and perfect will.

So when life seems hard, and you are being pounded and pushed almost beyond endurance; when your world seems to be spinning out of control; when you feel you're in a fiery furnace of trials; when life seems to "stink," of awful fumes, try this...

Brew a cup of your favorite tea, in your prettiest tea cup. Then sit down and think of this story and...have a little talk with the Potter.

(Author unknown)

Chapter 3

DEATH

Okay, you might say, that is pain and maybe all pain is an opportunity to grow closer to God. But what about death? Isn't death the termination of that opportunity? What about someone who dies young? How can that possibly be good?

Judaism assures us that this life is not the be all and end all. In fact, this life is only a "corridor" to the next world — which is the main realm of human existence. While this world is for seventy or eighty years, the next world is for eternity. This world is very much a side show to the main event.

Just like if life is about avoiding pain, there is no answer for why painful things happen, so too, if this world is the sum total of human existence, there is no answer for how people can die young.

In any case, both questions are meaningless outside of the context of God. For the atheist, the answer as to why bad things happen and people die young is simple, though perhaps uncomfortable. We live in a random world. And people die young because this random world does not distinguish between young and old. A falling tree or a cancer cell cannot and will not distinguish between someone who is good and someone who is bad, someone who has lived a full life and someone who has not. Only when we talk about God do these questions have any relevance. And if we are to ask these questions according to the axioms of monotheism, we must accept an answer in the same vein. And the concept of a next world is as axiomatic to monotheism as natural selection is to evolution.

I could, at this point, give a very simple, though deeply unsatisfying answer to our question of people dying young. I could merely say that death is not a bad thing because the soul goes to a better world. It is happier, more fulfilled, and has a deeper connection with God. In fact, pushing the idea to its extreme, one could say that death is just about the best thing that could happen to a person!

This is obviously not a satisfactory answer, because if death is so wonderful and should happen to everyone as soon as possible, why did God create us in this world in the first place? Why not put us all into the next world straight away?

In simple terms, this world is also good and leaving it "early" cannot be justified by a next world alone. I, for one, require a more sophisticated answer than this.

Dying Young

"And God saw that it was very good..." (Genesis 1:31). The Midrash (*Bereishis Rabbah* 9:12) asks what was created on the sixth day of creation that was "very good" versus the other five days which were only "good"? "Very good," it explains, refers to the angel of death. Death, in Judaism, is not only not very bad — it is actually very good. It is a very necessary element of this realm of existence, without which we would struggle to accomplish anything. And it's not good just because you go to a better world. It's a very good thing in and of itself.

Elana always used to say that if you lived forever, why would you bother to get up in the morning? You wouldn't need to accomplish anything today; you could always do it tomorrow. And if you didn't do it tomorrow, there would always be the next day. And if not the next day, you could do it in a thousand years or so. Why start your diet today when you can start it in ten thousand years? If life is forever, there's plenty of time for everything. Who needs to capture the moment — when there are an infinite amount of moments to be captured?

The fact that there is quite literally a "deadline" to life means that we have to get on with it. And the fact that the deadline is uncertain means that we cannot rely on tomorrow for accomplishment, because there may not be a tomorrow. Today is all that we have. The Rabbis tell us, "Return to reality one day before you die" (*Pirkei Avos* 2:15). How do you know which day is the one before you die? You don't, so do it today and every day. One of these days you will get it right!

Not knowing when we'll die creates, if we allow it to, a very real and healthy sense of urgency to get on with life.

Knowing when death is really imminent is something of a luxury. It focuses a person's attention in a way that nothing else can. I still vividly remember our oncologist calling me in to her office, six weeks before Elana died. The words she said, "Time is very short," are still etched in my memory. For the last six weeks of her life, when Elana knew that time was very, very short, she made use of every moment. And I made use of every moment with her. Our relationship was generally a very good one, but if we could have lived during our whole marriage the way we lived for those last six weeks, it would have been absolutely unbelievable. Unfortunately, the feeling that we have all the time in the world generates a certain sense of complacency. For six weeks, we were in no way complacent about our relationship. We didn't allow petty things to get in the way of our love for each other. And I look back on that time as being the time in my life when I was most alive. Elana felt the same way. Every second is always precious. But during those weeks, every second was not just precious but cherished.

So often, I wish that I could return to that deep and intimate experience of time being short. Reality has not changed, but illusion has taken over again. Time is as short for me now as it was for us then. If only I could feel it in the way I did during those six weeks, I know I would live my life very differently.

So the Rabbis are telling us that death is a wonderful reality that God has created in order to focus us on the goodness that we have right now. And they are, as always, careful in their language. They do not say that "death" is very good. They say that the "angel of death" is very good. The fact that we know there is an "angel of death" who will call upon us one day without necessarily ringing the bell first has the potential to wake us up to the goodness of life. It is not so much death that is good, but our awareness of death's certainty that is good. And it is not just "good." It is "very good."

Death, ironically, makes us wake up and live. And the fact that people die at various ages — some even very young — should make us realize that we can take nothing for granted. If everyone lived until ninety, we would not push ourselves at twenty or thirty or forty. We need death and we need the fact that people die young to remind us that the end can come at any moment. To remind us to live today in a way that we do not take tomorrow for granted.

But this is still not enough of an answer.

It might explain why some people die young, but still leaves us with a burning question as to why God chooses some and not others. And why does it so often seem that, as Billy Joel says, "Only the good die young"?

We have already dealt with two mistaken premises: First, that pain is bad and second, that death is bad. The former misleads us to believe that bad things do actually "happen" to good people. The latter misleads us to believe that when people die, we must question why God would do this to them.

To answer the final question of why specific people die at a young age, I need to bring in a third mistaken premise, which is that God owes us something; that there is a certain amount that is due a human being in this world and anything less is unfair.

Let's say that I give you $10,000. It is a free gift out of the goodness of my heart. I don't know you. You have done nothing to earn it.

What would you say to me? Or rather, what *should* you say to me? "Thank you very much," I would hope.

Okay, there you are feeling really good. I just gave you $10,000 as a present. And now I go over to your best friend and hand him $50,000. Again, I give it as a free gift — no strings attached. I don't know your friend any better than I know you and he has done as little as you to merit my kindness.

Now how do you feel about your $10,000? Not quite the same? Why did I only give you $10,000 when I gave your friend $50,000? Why is he more deserving than you are? All of a sudden, my $10,000 does not seem like the wonderful and generous gift that it was a few minutes ago.

This is plain and simple human nature. We don't judge what we have in absolute terms. We compare it to what others have. $10,000 is great — until my friend gets $50,000. Now my $10,000 looks like nothing, because of what I could (and in my mind, should) have been granted. And if I had been given the $50,000, I could also. As my friend whizzes by my brand new Mini in his brand new Porsche, my $10,000 seems almost like a curse.

It's crazy, but we all compare in this way. One of the great challenges of this world is to appreciate and enjoy what we ourselves have — even though there are others who have more.

This mistake of comparing to others is so pervasive and insidious that we often don't even notice just where and how much it is affecting us. We might not realize, but it is the main issue that bothers us when talking about why people die young.

What is "young"?

"Young" is a completely relative term that should have no real meaning when looking at the wonderful gift of life that we have been given.

The Bible says that people used to live a thousand years. Let's try to imagine a society in which that were the case — say that people usually died in their nine hundreds. Now, what would we say about a righteous man who died at one hundred years old? We would say it was terrible, a tragedy. He was cut down in his prime. We would ask ourselves the burning question — why do bad things happen to good people? And Billy Joel would write a song saying, "Only the good die young."

Let's take a look at the other side of the coin. In the Middle Ages, people used to live until thirty-five. So what would we say about someone who, like Elana, died at thirty? She lived to a ripe old age. She was blessed with a long and fruitful life.

The simple truth is that God owes us nothing — absolutely nothing. All He gives us is a free and wonderful gift. If we view the world with this in mind, it takes on a very different hue.

Life until now has been a gift. And every extra moment of life is another added gift. Be it one thousand years of extra moments or one hundred years of extra moments or thirty years or ten or five years, or five months or five weeks or even five days...each and every moment remains a gift. Every moment is precious. Every moment is special. Every moment is something to be thankful for, instead of complaining about the moments that we or others were not granted.

Why God might choose to give one person a larger gift than someone else is really not for us to ask. Even the smaller gift is still an incredible one — and is not in any way diminished by the fact that others get larger ones. God has every right to give one person a great deal and another person even more. It's not unfair. As the one giving, it's His prerogative to give as He sees fit. And for us to complain is an incredible lack of appreciation for the magnitude of what has been given to us in the first place. My previous analogy of $50,000 and $10,000 is completely understated. It is more like someone complaining that he was only given $10 billion, while his friend was given $50 billion.

Look at how ridiculous it is. We are observing an individual created by God. As a created being, he "deserves" nothing. But then, look! He is given ten billion dollars' worth of free gifts — he is given life, free will, emotions, a mind, family, friends, passion, arms and legs, vision, hearing, energy, talents...and the list goes on. And he is given all of these gifts for twenty-five whole years. Incredible! Do we respond by feeling that God is a wonderful giver? No, we complain that he got a raw deal. Only $10 billion instead of $50 billion? Really and truly, we are crazy.

This is the first point in my answer: it is wrong to question the giver of a gift as to whether it is large enough, because a gift is a good and blessed thing, no matter how small.

But there is another aspect, as well.

It may, in fact, be the case that all our gifts are exactly equal. Perhaps one person (Elana, for example) received a loftier soul and hence needed to spend less time in this world. Perhaps another person finished his or her task in this world and was ready to move on to a better place — which the next world surely is. Perhaps another person was given more material wealth, more intelligence, more love, but received less time. And yet another who did not receive these gifts was given more time instead. Who are we simple humans to know God's calculations?

Our children's favorite phrase is "It's not fair." Why did one get more than the other? Or even if they got the same, their friends got things that they didn't get. And even if they got more than their friends, still they did not get as much as they would have liked and it's all just so unfair. It's like a chorus in my house. I would estimate I hear it about twenty times a day. One of my many standard answers is as appropriate for this book as it is for my children. I will ask my sons, "If I were to buy your sisters a doll, would you want me to be perfectly fair and buy you one also?" And I ask my daughters, "If I bought your brothers a football, would you want one, as well?" Do they all want to wear diapers because the baby does? Of course not. Fair does not mean everyone getting exactly the same thing — it means each getting according to his or her particular needs. And this varies not just for male and female, young and old, but for every single individual. Even were I to feel (which I don't) that absolute equality was something important for my children, they would nevertheless end up with very different things.

The same concept of fairness is true for God. God metes out His blessings in perfectly equal measure to everyone. Not everyone gets the same, but everyone gets an equal amount of God's goodness. To judge fairness on one issue alone — that of length of life — is absurd.

Whether we are given one thousand minutes, days, weeks, months, or even years, it's fair. It's not the same, but it's fair and equal. Until we have all the facts in front of us, we will not be able to see it, but since God is the infinite being, we can trust He knows what He's doing and knows what is the ultimate fair deal.

As a final point on this topic, the Kabbalists talk about the concept of *gilgul neshamos* — reincarnation. This is the belief that for various reasons, souls might return to this world in new bodies. One of those reasons might be that they have accomplished a great deal in their past life, but still have more to do. They have not quite completed the task of "fixing" their soul. A short period of time in a new life would enable them to do so.

The Jewish concept is that the soul really does not want to be in this world in the first place. It would much rather be in the spiritual world that some call Heaven. It has a task to accomplish down here and it would rather be here for as short a time as possible. Maybe it only needs twenty years, or ten or five or maybe it only needs a few days or minutes in this world. If a person lived a short life, it might mean that they accomplished their mission and then moved on to a better world. It's only we who are left behind who feel the loss — not the one who died.

This is also one way of understanding a child who is born with Down's syndrome or any other similar condition. Their soul is one that has accomplished much and therefore needs less faculties to do what it now has to do. I heard it said that the Chazon Ish — possibly the greatest rabbi of the previous generation — used to stand up in respect if such a person walked into the room. He would say that they have a lofty soul and he wanted to show them due honor.

In summary of this section, pain is not bad. It is painful. Death is not bad. As a future certainty, it wakes us up to life. And when it happens, it takes us to a higher plane of existence. This world is one of frustration, challenge, difficulty, loss — but all of that leads us to the ultimate goal in this world, the attainment of Godliness. It's well worth it.

Dreams and Nightmares

Psalm 126, *Shir HaMaalos*, states that when the present exile comes to an end, "we will have been like dreamers." It will have been just a bad, albeit long, dream. Dreams are an amazing phenomenon — and a beautiful analogy for our life in this world. When you are in a dream, it all seems so real. You are not able to discern it as being illusion while you are experiencing it. As far as you are concerned, you are there and it is happening. Then you wake up. And suddenly, you realize that what you were experiencing was not real. You have no doubt that this is the case. You see it with complete clarity. As obviously real as it might have felt while you were in it, it is equally obviously unreal now that you are out of it.

This is especially true when the dream is a bad dream. It feels like you are really there. The nightmare is actually happening. You are being chased; you are falling; you are fighting; you are losing someone — whatever it might be. When you are within the nightmare, you do not understand it to be a dream. So you feel the terror, the horror, the pain. And then you wake up. The dream might linger momentarily, but very quickly, you realize that everything is okay. The nightmare was only a dream and the pain you felt was only an illusion. It's gone now, never to return. You relax immediately, and as quickly as it came, it is forgotten.

So too will it be, the Book of Psalms explains, with the exile of the Jewish people. The horror that the Jewish people has experienced during the last two thousand years — the torture, the inquisitions, the pogroms, the gas chambers, the suicide bombers...is a nightmare of the most massive proportions. But, the Rabbis explain, it is merely a nightmare. When the exile is over and the Jewish people are able to come close to God once again, when the good times finally arrive and the world returns to its state of perfection, the Jewish people, as a nation, will look back and feel it was all just a nightmare. When the world "wakes up," the dream will have vanished and the pain will be over — the purpose of it all will have been realized. Yes, it was painful at the time, but once it's over, the pain will be gone and forgotten.

This idea of the transience of pain is true not just on a national level, but also a personal level. The point is this: pain is only painful for as long as it exists. Pain never lingers — unless, of course, the situation lingers. The pain of losing Elana, for example, still remains with me not because the pain is lingering, but because Elana is still gone. Were she to miraculously return, the pain that I have would dissipate immediately. In the same way, if you break a leg and then it heals, you feel no more pain. The fact that you felt pain when it was broken will not remain with you once it is better.

This is a part of the nature of pain — it is temporary. It is not self-sustaining. It will only last as long as the circumstance that causes it lasts. After that it is as nonexistent as a nightmare. The only difference between real pain and a nightmare is that when you feel the pain it is real, whereas when you feel the nightmare it is not. Pain can maybe last much longer than a nightmare. Afterwards, however, both are gone in their entirety — as though they never existed.

It's true that a person can replay the nightmare in his head and re-experience it, remind himself of it, put himself back into it mentally and feel the horror once again. And this is true of pain also. People can torture themselves with something that is over and done with. They can cling to it and not let it go. But this ongoing pain is self-inflicted. It is not the natural way of the world. For one reason or another, a person can choose to allow the pain to linger, can choose to be the conduit that sustains the pain. This is, once again, human choice, and God will always allow us our free will. It may be incredibly difficult to let go, but we have the ability to do so. If we ourselves choose to hold on to pain, then we have no right to blame God that it still hurts.

We have all seen in our own lives the most painful of circumstances passing, and the pain disappearing as though it never existed. Think back to difficult and painful experiences you have had and see if remembering the pain bothers you at all. It is just a memory, perhaps a horrible memory, but it is not real. You can choose to let go of it.

The Talmud (*Niddah* 31b) gives us a clear example of how remembered pain does not have to affect us. It says that every woman who gives birth vows at some point during her labor that she will never do it again. The process is so painful that she cannot imagine repeating it. And yet, when the pain is gone, and all that remains is a beautiful new soul to love, women go through labor, over and over again, in order to have more children. I have never heard of a woman who really wants more children stopping after one child due to the pain of labor. Once the pain is gone, she is ready to try again.

Much more often than not, every pain we experience will pass in this world. But even if it does not, it will certainly pass in the next. The pains and difficulties of this world will fade as fast as a nightmare does — no matter how real and intense they are at the time. We are talking moments, perhaps minutes or days or months and perhaps even years of living with pain — versus an eternity with that pain gone. In the context of eternity, even a lifetime of pain will be forgotten very quickly.

And then, as *Shir HaMaalos* continues, "our mouths will be filled with laughter and our lips with song." The pain that the Jewish people felt for millennia will disappear so quickly that we will spontaneously laugh in relief and joy. So, too, on a personal level. When the pain goes, we can laugh and break into song. It seemed so real at the time, but now that it's gone, it's as if it never existed.

And that is the bottom line with pain. As real as it may seem when you are going through it, once it's gone, it's as though it never was. It's temporary. It passes. No pain lasts forever. If it does not pass in this world, it will certainly pass in the next.

Okay, you might say. Pain is not bad, it is "merely" painful. And pain is only real while it exists.

But still, it's a very unpleasant experience. Why did a loving God create the concept of pain in the first place and why is it so prevalent in His world — so much a part and parcel of everyday life?

Chapter 4

Dealing with Pain

Pain is part and parcel of the human experience. There is no one who does not experience real and serious pain during their lifetime. And that pain will be physical, emotional, and spiritual. Like it or not, and not liking it is without doubt our natural response, it is a reality of our existence.

It is not fair or true to say that some people go through more pain than others. Pain is all relative to the person experiencing it. My wife is able to have dental work done without anesthetic. I, on the other hand, cannot have a blood test without fainting. Pain is experienced differently by everyone and we cannot compare one person's pain to another's.

Pain is a given. And, as I have mentioned earlier, it is a wonderful given, for it enables us to connect to the infinite in a way that would otherwise be impossible.

Unfortunately, especially in our generation, pain can often be looked upon as the enemy, something to be avoided, not embraced. Such an attitude is a sure-fire road to mediocrity. No pain, no gain. Avoid pain and meaningful accomplishment becomes impossible. Of course, we don't go looking for pain, but avoiding it at all costs will only result in a society that misses out on much of the joy of life. A society that substitutes short-term thrills for real pleasures. A society like the one we live in today.

I often ask people what is the opposite of pain. Nine out of ten will immediately respond that it is pleasure. But when I press them to think more deeply, most appreciate that this is not the case. Think about it yourself before you continue. Is pleasure really the opposite of pain?

"Opposite" means diametrically opposed. They cannot exist together. You cannot have total dark and total light at the same time. Something cannot be alive and also dead. They are opposites and cannot coexist in the same object at the same point in time.

So now think about pain and pleasure for a minute. Can you experience pleasure while you are experiencing pain? When I go running, I reach a point where my eyes are stinging from the sweat running into them, my legs are aching, my lungs are bursting — every part of my body is crying out for me to give up. And yet I carry on — and I love it! It's not masochism, it's the great pleasure I take in overcoming pain. It's pain and pleasure coexisting. The marathon runner who crosses the finish line is in absolute agony — and at the same time absolute ecstasy.

Pain and pleasure are not opposites.

The opposite of pain is, in fact, no pain. A total feeling of comfort. Pain and comfort cannot coexist. The marathon runner might experience deep pleasure, but he is not comfortable. He is in pain. It is impossible to be in pain and at the same time be comfortable. You are only comfortable to the extent that you are not in pain and only in pain to the extent you are not comfortable.

Pleasure, on the other hand, is something very different. We can experience pleasure, not in spite of pain, but because of it.

Had the marathon runner been given a drug to make running a marathon as easy as walking down the street, he would experience no pleasure whatsoever in crossing the finish line. Pain is an absolute necessity in order to experience true pleasure. As I said earlier, no pain, no gain.

People will put themselves through inordinate amounts of pain in order to experience pleasure. Rabbi Weinberg often gives a very simple example. Imagine you took twenty-two men and told them to play soccer for ninety minutes — only without a ball. They are to run around, tackle each other, kick, head, do all the things that one does when the ball is there, only the ball's not there! After ten minutes, they would be exhausted and unable to continue. The pain alone would be too much, without the pleasure of the game alongside it.

But once you throw a ball onto the field, everything changes. The same twenty-two men will run around like lunatics, jump, dive, puff, and pant — and absolutely love it. The great effort of the game is precisely what makes it pleasurable.

To define pleasure as the opposite of pain is incredibly misleading. Because in doing so, we associate pleasure with comfort (the true opposite of pain). And this simple misdefinition has very, very significant ramifications. If pain is the opposite of pleasure — and of course pleasure is what we are all striving for — then pain must be avoided at all costs. Comfort becomes the be all and end all, and the search for one's ultimate good becomes the search for the easiest and most comfortable existence. In doing this, we may provide ourselves with lifestyles that are basically pain free, but they will never be filled with deep and lasting pleasure, because "no pain, no gain" is an inescapable reality of our existence.

For example, many people are wary of the pain, effort, and expense involved in raising a large family. Some opt to avoid having children altogether. Life may be easier, but the new pleasure that comes with each child and the amazing satisfaction that comes from a large family's loving devotion and interconnections are completely missed.

Instead of the challenge and struggle of marriage, some couples opt out by living together; they avoid the risks, but also miss out on the depth of relationship that only total commitment can engender. Married couples are forced to confront issues head on, rather than sidestepping any unpleasantness. And only by dealing with issues do relationships deepen to their fullest extent. Living together is certainly easier — but the effort of marriage is what brings the deeper pleasure.

And what happens when people do get married and then go through a rough spot (as happens at times in every good marriage)? Do they take on the painful work of developing the relationship, or do they choose the easier, though much less fulfilling, route of simply giving up and finding another partner? Moving on to another relationship when your present one becomes too challenging might be the easier, more "comfortable" choice, but it also guarantees that you will never reach a deeply fulfilling level in any of your relationships.

Instead of investing in our relationship with our children, do we put them in front of the television? Do we avoid the pain of spending time with them, but miss out on the pleasure of their youth?

At its extreme, this attitude undermines the very fabric of our society. Because instead of taking on the pain of standing up for what they believe in, people will choose the easier option of not really believing in anything. Absolute morality is a strain that a society bent on avoiding pain will make sure to avoid. So we end up with the state of affairs that exists today. Stand up for nothing other than the right of yourself and others to avoid the restrictions of absolute values — in other words, stand up only for your own right to continue avoiding pain as best you can. Nowadays, it's only worth going through pain if you avoid greater pain in doing so.

Of course, there is a very deep problem inherent with this whole approach. It's not just that avoiding pain means that we do not experience pleasure. Maybe some would actually choose that for themselves. The problem is that it just doesn't work, because avoiding the more superficial pains actually causes the deepest pain of all. As beings made in the image of God, our deepest pain is distance from Him. All other pains are transient, but this one is eternal. And so, by avoiding the pain of the moment, we condemn ourselves to a pain that will remain with us for eternity. By avoiding the struggle towards Godliness, we ensure that our lot is one of spiritual emptiness. How many television programs and movies can we watch? How much can a person run from one superficial high to the next until the hollowness of such an existence finally catches up with him? And even if he does manage to run for seventy years, in the grave there will be nowhere to run.

The only way to find what we are looking for is by facing and overcoming pain. This is a world of challenge, and the more we are able to overcome that challenge, the more we will achieve and the more pleasure, goodness, and Godliness we will attain.

Facing and overcoming pain is what life is about.

Elana and I developed many strategies for dealing with pain, for making sure that pain was something that lifted us into God and didn't just make us bitter and resentful. These strategies are ultimately my purpose in writing this book. It is my sincere hope that the reader will find them as useful as I have and still do.

Chapter 5

Strategy 1: Hashgachah, Divine Providence

Moshe is late for a meeting and is desperately looking for a parking space in downtown Manhattan. As he's driving around in circles, he starts to pray, "Please, God, open up a parking space for me and I will daven with more *kavanah*, spend more time with my wife, and learn more seriously."

No sooner does he finish the sentence than a parking space miraculously appears right in front of him.

Moshe looks towards Heaven and says, "Not to worry, God. I already found one for myself."

The Sages tell us, "When a man sees troubles coming upon him, he should examine his deeds. If he can find nothing that warrants such pain, he should assume it is due to *bitul Torah* [neglect of Torah study]" (*Berachos* 5a). I understand the concept of *bitul*

Torah over here to mean that he may not be doing anything bad, but by the same token, he may not be putting in the proper effort to accomplish all that he is able to accomplish in his life. What I wish to focus on here, though, is the first part of the *gemara.*

I have often heard it said that we cannot understand why Hashem causes us pain — why He makes "bad" things happen to us. He has His reasons and who are we to try to understand? We can only trust that He knows what He's doing to us and get on with our lives.

This is actually an incredibly anti-Jewish attitude and another manifestation of our society's insistence on avoiding pain at all costs. In this case, it means avoiding the pain of trying to understand where we have gone wrong, avoiding the pain of taking responsibility for our mistakes, and, finally, avoiding the pain of facing the problem and changing our course of action. There is a lot of pain-avoiding going on here, and hence this is a hot and heavy topic for many people. It seems that the more a concept helps avoid pain, the more zealously people will defend it.

This seemingly innocuous point — that pain comes because of mistakes we have made — can cause incredible resistance and even anger on the part of many people. People love to challenge me with an extreme example, saying, "Who are you to say the Holocaust happened because of the 'sins' of the victims? What about the holy and righteous people? What about the children?"

This conclusion, of course, is a complete non-sequitur. It is not at all what I am saying. But when we are dealing with so emotionally charged an issue, due to the high level of pain-avoidance, I have learned that it is sometimes incredibly difficult for a person not to allow their feelings to confuse the issue.

The Gemara is clear and unequivocal. If troubles come upon a person, the very first assumption he must make is that he has been doing something wrong. The troubles come, not as a punishment, but as a wake-up call. If he sees that he has done nothing to warrant this level of pain (see *Rashi* on the Gemara), then he must move on to the assumption that he is simply not struggling enough in life, not pushing forward as much as he could, not reaching his potential to grow spiritually.

Were it to be the case that we cannot know the reason that pain happens to us, the Gemara should have said something very different. It should have said, "When a person sees troubles coming upon him, he should trust in God and know that there is a good reason for it." The Gemara does not say this. It says that he should look into his deeds.

Even if you say that sometimes we can figure out the reason for our pain and sometimes we can't, the next part of the Gemara disproves this: "If he can find nothing that warrants such pain, he should assume it is due to *bitul Torah*."

If it were true that sometimes we just can't know, the Gemara should not instruct us to take a next step — it should merely say that if you cannot figure out the answer, it must be one of those cases in which you don't know. But this Gemara never says that. It gives an answer for every scenario.

We can know and we must know why things happen to us.

There is a wonderful illustration of this in the Torah portion of *Mikeitz*.

Joseph was sold by his brothers and taken down to Egypt. He was gone for over twenty years. As far as they were concerned, he was dead.

Now the brothers are faced with a famine in the land of Canaan and they, themselves, must go down to Egypt to find food. They enter the land and are immediately brought before the Egyptian viceroy (not knowing that he is Joseph). They explain to him that they are seeking food, and he accuses them of being spies. The only way he will allow them to go back home is if one of the brothers remains behind as a hostage, and if they promise to come back to Egypt with the youngest brother.

Troubles clearly are coming upon them. They are dealing with the most powerful man in the world, and he obviously has it in for them. What is the response of these great men in such a time of difficulty?

It is immediate and unequivocal. They say to each other, "We are guilty in that we saw our brother's pain and did not listen. And so this trouble has befallen us" (Genesis 38:21).

There is no discussion of how to operate in a pragmatic sense. Do they talk the viceroy out of it? Do they pay him off? Their first and foremost response is a purely spiritual one. We are in trouble and therefore it must be a message from God. What could the message be? It is obvious to all of them — we sold our brother into slavery of our own free will and now this Egyptian is demanding another brother by force. Measure for measure. The hand of Providence is clear. And the brothers are quick to read it correctly and respond to it — as a Jew always should.

It is clear and obvious from the Gemara and from the response of Joseph's brothers that the Torah believes we can know the reason painful things happen to us, and if we want to respond properly, we must make the effort to figure it out.

Far from being a horrible thought, this is actually an incredibly empowering concept. And, as such, it is our first tool in dealing with pain.

If, as discussed earlier, pain is there for us to grow, then we need to know in which area God wants us to grow — otherwise our pain is completely and utterly meaningless. Why would God send us a message — but send it in Chinese? If you had an important message to send your children, so important that you felt it necessary to put them through pain in order to get it across, would you send it in a foreign language?

Imagine that a parent sends his child to his room and when the child asks why, he says he's not going to tell him and the child won't be able to figure it out, either. It would be completely pointless. It would be a form of torture for a child to be reprimanded without being given any opportunity to identify the mistake and correct it.

I have sometimes heard people say that pain is not really a message, but rather a medium — that the pain, in and of itself, corrects us. We don't need to figure out the reason and learn from it; we just need to go through the difficult experience, and in doing so we will change.

It is obvious to me that this is not only incorrect, but contradicts Jewish belief on the most fundamental level. It means that God is denying us our free will. The concept that we make mistakes and God corrects them through pain distinctly sounds like another religion far removed from our own. In Judaism, free will is a given. We are not robots; we are independent beings. God will not force us to change; but He will give us opportunity and guidance so that we can choose to either change or not, as we wish. Pain cannot be something that changes us automatically, for that would mean God changing us rather than we changing ourselves. Pain can only be a conduit to direct us to make our own changes. But in order to do so, we must understand the message and make the decisions accordingly.

The fact that we can understand our own pain and change accordingly is incredibly empowering. Because if God is doing something we cannot understand, then we are mere puppets. We have no control of the outcome. In that case, pain is simply a roller coaster ride and all we can do is hold on tight. If, however, we can understand what is happening, then we can change it. We made the mess and we can clean it up. We are masters of our own destiny.

I do not say this in a glib fashion. For a father to subject his children to pain, there must be something very wrong. And you do not correct something very wrong in an easy and quick way. We can find an example in the book of Esther. The Jews wrongly attended the banquet of King Achashveirosh. They should not have participated in the affair of an evil man. Not long after, Haman is appointed prime minister of Persia and given the king's signet ring. He now has not only the will but also the power to bring about the utter annihilation of the Jewish people.

The Rabbis tell us that when Haman received the royal seal, the Jews of Shushan understood immediately what they had done wrong. They fasted three days and returned to God. In response, God overturned the decree for their destruction. It required a gargantuan response from the Jewish people — but it worked. So too, with a similar level of response and responsibility, an individual can overturn a personal decree. It's not easy — but it can be done.

It is possible to understand and to change and to take away the pain. We are in complete control of our destiny. This is the reality of free will. And it's a beautiful thing.

Let me not be misunderstood. Pain is a message for the individual. A number of people may experience the same pain, the same disease or calamity, but it might be a very different message for each. The message is always intensely personal. As such, although a person can understand a message that is given to him, he can in no way assume to understand the message given to another. He can speculate, he can advise, but he can never "know" the reason. Only the person going through the pain can decide the purpose for it — for only he or she can know him- or herself well enough to know the mistakes which have been made and where they have stemmed from. Pain is an incredibly intimate and personal aspect of God's relationship with us, one to which others are not necessarily privy.

Because we cannot understand the reasons for the pain of others, it is not for any of us, for example, to try to find a reason for the suffering of the individuals who went through the Holocaust. It did not happen to us and so we cannot make any sort of judgment. But there is a reason. And each survivor has the ability to understand how God spoke to him during that horrific time.

At the time of the prophets, things were different. When a person was ill, instead of going to a doctor, he would go to a prophet, who would tell him via divine inspiration the reason for his illness. Without prophets today, we have only ourselves to rely on. One might feel this is a daunting task, but we can always reach an understanding. For the more daunting the task, the greater the level of Heavenly assistance we receive. A person in the time of the prophets would not have been able to figure it out for himself — for he did not need to do so. We, who can be seen as "spiritual orphans," are given the capacity.

There is no question that it helps to get advice from others on the issue, to discuss with friends, spouses, and certainly rabbis. They can give advice and they can help confirm conclusions we might reach. But ultimately, in the absence of prophets, the individual must take a deep breath of trust in Hashem and draw his own conclusion.

When Elana and I understood this, we felt infinitely better. We could know the reason and we could change. And we could turn the decree around.

Why then, you might ask, did she die? As I have explained, that is a question that only I can answer for myself — and I have my answers. I have shared much and will share more, but this far I am unwilling to go. Suffice it to say, it poses no philosophical problem for me. It poses pain — incredible pain, but no doubt. And, thankfully, no guilt.

How Do You Do It?

It's all very well to say that you can know, but how do you go about figuring it out? What is the mechanism for doing so? Let me start with an idea that was of significant help to Elana and me in getting this concept into our bones.

I often find that people are great at seeing where God "is not" in our lives. But we are not so great at seeing just where He "is." When things go wrong, we usually ask, "Where was God? Why did He allow this to happen to us?" Rarely, however, when things go right, do we give Him the credit for working things out.

How often will we give God the credit when a business deal goes well or when we find what we were looking for in the first shop we enter, or even when we easily find a parking space? It's only fair that if God is going to take the rap when problems arise, He should also get the credit when things go well. He's either in control or not. It can't be that He's in control when things go wrong, but we're in control when they go right!

It stands to reason that if we have a distorted and unfair picture of God's involvement in our lives, we will have difficulty putting into perspective that which causes us pain.

It's like a parent-child relationship. The extent to which the child feels confident of his parent's love is the extent to which he can be accepting of his rebuke. A child who doubts his parent's love will respond negatively to any reprimand. But a child who feels a deep sense of love from his parents will surely respect them when they make decisions which cause him pain. As long as he knows that they're on his side, he will be able to handle whatever they throw at him.

The same is true of our relationship with God. We need to know that God is on our side if we are to relate to him properly during the difficult times. And the time to feel that God is on our side is when things are good. If we work on that feeling during the good times, we will have a "friend" during the hard times. But if we fail to feel God's love when all is going our way, we will certainly not feel it when we go through pain.

When Elana first became ill, Rabbi Weinberg gave us a suggestion that really helped us focus on God's love for us. He suggested that on Friday night, we tell "*hashgachah* stories." Stories of how, during the past week, we saw God's hand in our lives. It might have been something as simple as finding a parking space right outside the store or being late for a train and finding that the train was also late. "Look for God in your life and you will find Him," was the principle. And it worked wonders for us. It has long been an integral part of our Friday night experience. Our children love finding stories in the week where God was clearly a part of their lives (and the treat they get for coming up with a story certainly helps). This gets the whole family in touch with the fact that God is here with us on a daily basis.

As a result of five years of doing this, we have become a family that very much recognizes God's direct and ongoing involvement in our lives. Over and over again, events will happen during the week and our children (even our four-year-old) will point out the *hashgachah* in what happened. If we find money in the street, the first thing our children shout out is, "Wow, *hashgachah*!" It's not a random happening and it's not luck. It's God giving us a gift.

I want to share my two favorite examples: My sister-in-law needed to get a train home one day. She put her money into the ticket machine, but just as she did, she realized she did not have enough cash. Here she was, stuck in Central London, where she didn't know a soul! She pushed the cancel button to get her money back, and when she picked up the change, she saw the ticket machine had given her back more than she had originally put in! And it was exactly the correct amount of money for her ticket!

But my favorite story of all came from my five-year-old son. One Friday night, he related that he had just opened a bottle of fizzy drink at the table. It had been shaken up, so it squirted out all over the place. But, by *hashgachah*, it was pointing in the right direction. Not a drop went on him. It went all over his little sister instead!

Hashgachah stories are a way of bringing an awareness of God into your daily life. The more you see God's hand in everything, the easier it will be to see His hand and feel His love in the pain, too.

These stories will help put you in the frame of mind that when pain comes, instead of becoming angry and frustrated that life is not going your way, you can, as the rabbis say, examine your deeds and understand what God is saying to you. With *hashgachah* stories helping us approach our trials with a proper perspective, let's discuss how one actually goes about finding a message in the pain.

A friend and colleague, Rabbi Moshe Mayerfeld, gave the analogy of sitting across the room from someone who's trying to signal something to you. They mouth what they are trying to say, make signs, jump up and down, and you just don't get the point. Now take the same scenario with your spouse or a close friend across the room. They can wink an eye or wave a hand and you immediately get it. The closer you are to someone, the easier it is to understand the message they are communicating.

So, too, with God. For those who are close, the meaning of the message comes relatively easily. For those of us who are a little farther away, we have to work a lot harder.

As with anything in life, however, practice makes perfect. I can teach you to play tennis in ten minutes — forehand, backhand, serve, smash, lob, spin, the works... But now let's see you get the ball over the net! There are no magic formulas that will work immediately. You just have to have patience and give it time and effort. And you'll get frustrated and feel you're not progressing at first — as with anything new. But I guarantee this — persevere as you would with tennis, and in a relatively short period of time, you'll get the hang of it.

The following tips are not the only tools you can use. These are ideas that have helped me, and so I share them with you. There are many other approaches. You just need to get your feet wet.

1. Middah Keneged Middah

The Rabbis tell us that God responds to us "measure for measure" (*Sanhedrin* 90a). The nature of the response arises directly from the nature of the mistake. The purpose of this is to help us get the message. A simplistic example would be if you speak badly of another person, instead of tripping and hurting your foot, you might bite your tongue. If you punch a person, you might have an ache in your hand. These examples are oversimplifications, but thinking along simple lines can help solve the more complex cases.

It's best to always start with the obvious because God usually talks to us in a very simple and straightforward way. Don't look for more complex correlations until you have to.

So let's take some simple examples, starting with hurting your leg. Ask first, "What might I have done wrong with my legs? Have I been running to do things I should not be doing? Did I kick someone — either literally or metaphorically?" If you hurt your eye, ask what you have been looking at that you should not have. Have you been wasting too much time watching television or maybe seeing people in pain and not responding with sensitivity? If your children are driving you crazy, ask yourself how you have been bringing them up.

Usually, if you come up with an idea that fits, it will immediately feel right. But that doesn't always happen. Sometimes, you have to come up with a few possibilities and spend some time in honest introspection in order to see what seems right.

Hopefully, this type of thinking will be enough to begin to understand the message and make the changes necessary. If, however, you draw a blank at this simpler level, you'll need to gradually take your thinking deeper.

Let's say you lose a lot of money. The first ports of call might be, "Have I been responsible with my money or have I been wasting it? Have I been giving enough to charity, been generous enough, or have I been hoarding it for myself?" Being that the answer to both of these questions is probably that you could have done more, you now face the challenging part. You have to call upon your intuition to evaluate if this message fits the mistake. Do you feel that the amount of money you lost and the amount of pain that it has caused you is commensurate with your level of irresponsibility or lack of giving? It's a question that only you can answer; a question that if you sincerely try, God will surely help you to answer.

It certainly takes great courage to trust your judgment. But at worst it will lead you to think you need to change in an area that you probably do need to change — but is not the exact point of the message. Not trusting your judgment, however, will lead you to learning nothing from the experience at all! Let's say, for example, you experience a financial setback and come to the conclusion that you are not giving enough charity. And let's say that this is the wrong message; God is trying to tell you to be more generous with your own family. So now you are giving more to charity, but still being stingy with your family. Not so terrible — at least you changed something from the experience. You have grown. And by becoming more giving to others, you may eventually become less tight with your own family's expenses also.

But if you simply say that you cannot know why these troubles have come upon you, now what are you left with? You don't grow in any area at all.

At least when you make a judgment, you are grappling with the issue and moving forward. In addition, there is a principle from the Talmud that "The one who comes to purify, God helps him" (*Shabbos* 104a). Surely, your sincere desire to understand where you are going wrong and to change counts for something in God's eyes. Surely He is not going to let you make a mistake if you're trying your best to be honest and objective. And if you do somehow make a mistake, at least you have made your best effort.

Let's take the process a little further.

Let's say that you've done all the above, but you still can't figure it out. You honestly feel that the amount of money you lost cannot have been due to either lack of giving or irresponsibility.

Now you need to work a little harder. You need to move beyond the simple answers and start to look at things that aren't quite as obvious. What are the consequences of your losing this money? It's humbling. You will have to rely more on God. Maybe you were getting too big for your boots. Or maybe you were trusting too much in money, thinking you were in control. Or maybe you were being overly concerned with money in your relationship with your spouse. Perhaps money had become too big a part of your life. Perhaps you spend too much time thinking about money.

Perhaps, perhaps, perhaps…

You might think the options are endless. But they are not. The reason they seem endless in this hypothetical scenario is precisely because it is not real. But when you are dealing with a real-life situation, the possibilities are limited. You can know if it's arrogance or being too focused on money or irresponsibility, for example, because you can see if it's the case. You will quickly eliminate many possibilities and leave yourself with a few prime suspects.

It's not as difficult as it sounds. The danger does not lie in being unable to figure it out nor in coming to the wrong conclusion. The danger lies in giving up because the task seems so daunting. Those people, and they are many, who give up before they even start, make the incomprehensibility of God's messages into a self-fulfilling prophecy.

If you give it a go, you'll find it's easier than it sounds. And once you become proficient, it'll be like driving a car. If you're brave enough to get behind the wheel in the first place, you can be pretty certain you'll soon be driving.

2. Begin from the Other Direction

Sometimes the first approach can be a little too clinical and direct. It might be easier to start with the mistakes you've been making in life. Is there any major mistake you may be making that God might wish to draw your attention to? Do any of these fit with what is going on in your life? It may not always be in terms of measure for measure, but in terms of magnitude of mistake versus magnitude of what has gone wrong.

This is not quite as "scientific" as the first approach, but it may be easier. The means do not really matter as long as one gets to some sort of conclusion at the end of it all.

3. External Advice

How about asking someone who is close to you — a rabbi, a family member, a friend?

You could ask within the context of the particular "bad" thing that is happening to you. Or you could just ask them in general: Where do they feel you are making mistakes? Where could you improve as a person?

As I said before, only you can fully know the answer, but others can help lead you there. Once you hear their input, you will still have to rely on your own judgment to choose that which makes sense and discard the rest.

It can be a mistake to go to a rabbi and simply take his answer as being the correct one. God is talking to you, not to him. He can advise and suggest, but he cannot decide for you. There are simply no shortcuts to the daunting task of understanding what God is telling us.

Go to a rabbi for advice and go to him for confirmation. But don't go to him because you don't want to have to think.

4. Prayer

Prayer is not a solution in and of itself, but it can certainly help. God knows why He is putting you through this challenge and He could easily give you the answer. Ask God to help you understand. Ask Him to help you make the right judgments and draw the right conclusions.

Without doubt, He wants you to learn the lessons He is teaching you. Why else would He bother sending these messages? But He wants to be sure that you are really ready to hear. Prayer shows Him that you are serious.

There are many other ways and methods to find answers. You have to work out what is right for you. The key elements are simply not to be daunted by the task and to trust your judgment — for it is all you have.

With honesty and effort, we can know what God is telling us and change accordingly. And in so doing, we can turn that which is seemingly bad into something that is very obviously good.

Chapter 6

Strategy 2: Happiness

Count Your Blessings

This is something that Elana and I did together until she lost consciousness for the final time. And it is something that I still do today without her.

Simply said, if you appreciate the goodness of life, then when the challenges come, you have a healthy emotional context with which to face them.

If a person is depressed, problems will only depress him more. If he is just barely hanging on to happiness, problems may push him over the edge. But if he lives with the reality of life being a most wondrous experience, he'll be much more able, not only to ride the storm, but even to view it in a positive light.

Sounds easy, hey? Just feel that life is fantastic and life will be fantastic. Now why hasn't every therapist since Freud come up with so marvelously simple an approach to the challenges of life?

Well, there is one small and obvious problem. Just how exactly do you go about getting yourself to feel that life is fantastic in the first place?!

I can tell you that Elana was able to get there. I still remember her waking up in the middle of the night, a few days before she died. She could hardly speak, due to her serious lack of breath, but she desperately wanted to communicate. Finally, when she got the words out, she simply wanted to say, while beaming her big smile, "I am so incredibly blessed." She didn't feel this way before she got cancer. It was something she worked on and changed within herself in the midst of her illness.

To understand how, we need to look at how we view happiness.

People think that happiness is a happening. Either we are or we're not. They think it depends on a number of factors — personality, life experience, circumstance, certain chemical balances within our bodies… There seems to be a general consensus that whether or not we are happy is something that is beyond our control.

Judaism does not believe this to be the case. Judaism believes that happiness, far from being a happening, is something that we are in control of. And because it is something we can control, it is an actual obligation: "*Mitzvah gedolah lihiyos besimchah*" (*Likutei Maharan, Mahadura Basra*, siman 24). Being happy is an obligation to yourself, to those around you, and to God. Let's take each one separately for a moment.

1. An Obligation to Yourself

Simply stated, happy people accomplish more in life.

Take something mundane like getting up in the morning. Generally, a happy person will wake up early and with vigor, whereas a depressed person will struggle to drag himself out of bed. Depressed people can sleep sixteen hours, and more, a day if they allow themselves to do so — and still feel tired afterwards. Happy people can usually get by with much less sleep. Happy people will also be more successful in their relationships with others, if only because no one wants to hang out with someone who's miserable. Happy people will usually not be daunted by challenging tasks and will deal with failure in a much healthier way. A happy person will take failure in stride, whereas a miserable person may be crushed further by failure — or respond with bitterness and anger.

If only for the effect on your own life, Judaism says that happiness is an obligation. But there is more...

2. An Obligation to Others

Our state of happiness has a very significant effect on those around us. As I just mentioned, no one wants to hang out with someone miserable. But it goes much further than that. In the story of Cain and Abel, we see a model for all future human relationships. Cain's offering to God is not accepted, whereas Abel's is. Cain becomes depressed as a result. God tells him to pick himself up, but Cain chooses to wallow in his misery. The Torah tells us what happened next: "And it was, when they were in the field and Cain said to Abel and he struck him and killed him" (Genesis 4:8).

Even in English, this is clearly an incorrect usage of the verb "to say." The word "say" in English, as in Hebrew, needs a definite object. When you say that someone "said," you also have to say what he said. The rabbis explain the reason the Torah leaves out the object of the sentence. It's irrelevant what Cain actually said to Abel. He said something to him. He picked a fight. He found an excuse. The point is not what he said, but the fact that he looked for and found a reason to start an argument.

The message is clear to us. Violence in general has little to do with the circumstance of the violence and much more to do with the state of mind of the perpetrator. Cain was upset with his own life, so he killed his brother Abel.

Happy people are very rarely violent members of society. They might be driven to crime by necessity, but violence is not their thing. I have often heard Rabbi Weinberg ask, "Who would you rather be mugged by? A happy mugger or a miserable mugger?" Think about it for a moment. The miserable mugger will take all your money and give you a kick for good measure. The happy mugger will mug you with a smile, apologize, but explain that he needs food for his family. Then he'll probably give you bus fare home.

Happiness makes a difference on every level. Near my office I have a choice of a few stores that sell drinks. In one of them, there used to work an incredibly happy man. He always had a smile on his face and served you with real joy. Sometimes he would sing as he worked. Even though this store was actually farther away than the others, I would always go there, because I felt uplifted by him. And whenever I mentioned the happy guy to others in my office, they immediately knew who I was talking about and smiled when they pictured him.

Happiness is infectious. So is misery. Our state of happiness affects those around us so much that Judaism makes it our responsibility to be happy.

3. An Obligation to God

Imagine you give someone one thousand dollars as a gift. The next day you come into their house and find them burning the notes in the fire. They aren't really interested in money, so they're burning it for fun.

How would you feel?

You would probably feel upset and angry. You gave them your hard-earned money. At the very least, they should use it and enjoy it. We expect people to enjoy what we give them. If they throw it back in our faces, we will quickly lose the incentive to give more.

This is particularly true of parents. If you ask most good parents what they really want from their children, they will say that at least their children should be happy. It is agony for parents to see their children unhappy. Parents want to give to their children, and if their children are unable to appreciate what is being given, it undermines the whole purpose of parenthood.

God is no different.

In Jewish thinking, He is our Father in Heaven. He wants us to be happy. He gives us goodness so that we will be happy. The very basic minimum that we "owe" Him is to enjoy and take pleasure in the goodness that He has given us and continues to give us every moment.

He loves us and wants us to be happy. If we are not, it is as if, so to speak, He is wasting His time.

The effect that our state of happiness has on ourselves, others, and even, so to speak, God, is significant indeed. It extends far beyond the simple issue of whether or not we will be able to get up in the morning. It is not just a "mitzvah," an obligation. It is a "*mitzvah gedolah*," a great obligation — for its ramifications are far-reaching.

But once again, we need to be practical. We are obliged to be happy, and God can only obligate us if it is within our power.

So how do we do it?

Working on Happiness

The first step is to realize a very simple universal reality. No matter how difficult life is, no matter what situation a human being finds himself in, he is nevertheless incredibly blessed. Each and every one of us has so much to appreciate. Even in the most trying of circumstances, life is still full of almost infinite goodness.

The mistake we make is to focus on what we don't have and ignore just how much we do have.

I often use the following example when I teach a class on this topic.

I ask a person how he would feel if he just won ten million dollars in the lottery. Would he have a big grin on his face? Would he be skipping down the street, singing as he went? Most people answer that they surely would.

Okay, I continue, we're doing some medical research and we need a fresh leg to experiment on. We're willing to pay you ten million dollars for one of your legs. It's a painless operation, over in an hour, and you'll hop out of the hospital ten million dollars richer. We'll even throw in the latest prosthetic as a freebie. There may be the odd person who would take me up on the offer, but most people decline.

Okay, I continue, you won't take ten million dollars for one of your legs? That means you possess something more valuable than a mere ten million dollars. In fact, you have two of them! And you wouldn't give up your arms either, nor your eyes, nor your tongue, nor your hearing, nor your emotions, nor your independence, nor any of at least five family members... The list goes on. In fact, when you add it all up, every single human being — no matter what his circumstance — has gifts that he himself would value at billions. We are all billionaires! And most of us are miserable billionaires, at that!

It doesn't make sense. If we would skip down the street for just ten million dollars of lottery money, why then are we not skipping down the street for being multibillionaires?

It comes from a quirk in human nature.

We are always striving for more, which, in and of itself, is not a bad thing. That's the part of us that drives us towards Godliness, the part that will lift us quite literally to the heavens. However, a problem arises. In order to achieve more, we must focus on what we do not yet have. And focusing on that which we lack can very easily make us forget just how much we do have. Unless we make a conscious effort to focus on what we are blessed with, we can have a life full to the brim of goodness — and walk around miserable because of a toothache.

There is a classic example in the book of Esther. Haman, the evil prime minister of the Persian Empire, is riding on the crest of not just a wave, but a tidal wave. He is the wealthiest man in the world. He is the most powerful man in the world. He is the most respected and honored man in the world. He has ten wonderful sons who idolize him and a wife who adores him. The whole world bows to him — all, that is, except for one man, Mordechai the Jew. And so, Haman is miserable. He says to Zeresh, his wife, that all his wealth, all his honor, all his power means nothing to him, as long as Mordechai does not bow down (Esther 5:11–13). He has it all, but really he has nothing. He is so obsessed with Mordechai that he can think of nothing else. But Mordechai is not his problem. If Mordechai had bowed down to him, you can be sure he would have found something else to irritate him — his sick hamster or his inability to play the mouth organ. It doesn't matter what it is. When you don't focus on what you have and enjoy it, something along the way will make you miserable.

I do a fair amount of fund-raising and it's always amazing to me that some of the wealthiest people I meet are also some of the most unhappy people I meet. They may know how to make money, but they certainly don't know how to enjoy it.

It's simple human nature to focus on what we do not have, more so than on what we do have. In a certain way, it drives the world forward — especially in a capitalist society. There is a whole advertising industry whose sole purpose is to remind us constantly of what we lack. They want to remind us that even though we have last year's Porsche, it does not in any way compare to this year's. Why be happy with the Porsche that makes you plain coffee when you could have the one that makes you cappuccino? Why be happy sitting in your office working hard when you could be sunning on a beach in Hawaii?

It's a sure-fire formula for an unhappy society.

Judaism defines happiness as taking pleasure in the goodness that exists in your life. Misery is getting caught up with the goodness that you don't have but wish you did. And every single day, we are bombarded with messages telling us that what we have is just not as good as what we could — and really should — have. Under such circumstances, it makes it so difficult to discover true happiness.

But it's not impossible and I'll give you a few ideas that might help you along.

Saying Thank You

How do you get yourself to focus on what you do have, as opposed to what you don't?

I'll give you two ideas that helped Elana and me a great deal in changing our perspective on life and hence on our situation.

The general principle is "just do it." Just start focusing on what you have and start forcing into your consciousness how blessed you really are.

First, Elana and I did what we called "Thank You, Hashem's." Every day we would try to do this five times at regular intervals and ideally together — face to face or over the phone. If we couldn't do it together, we would do it separately.

We would thank God for five good things that had happened during the last few hours. Let's say we would do this first at 10 a.m., so this might be how it would go — "Thank You, Hashem, for a delicious breakfast this morning and thank You for loving me." Ideally, we would try to make the pleasure more real by describing it and savoring it with each other — the corn flakes were crunchy and tasted nutritious. I enjoyed the sensation of crunching them between my teeth and chewing them. The milk was cold and felt good in my throat. The sugar gave me a sweet sensation.

"Thank You, Hashem, for giving me a wonderful two minutes with my son this morning and thank You for loving me. I loved the way that he smiled at me so warmly and I was able to give him the answer he needed for his homework and he went off to school so excited and full of joy. I loved his happiness and his energy so early in the morning."

"Thank You, Hashem, for the cold fresh air this morning. I loved the way I felt more awake and alive when I went out, the way that the cold air felt fresh and energizing, the crispness of the cold winter's day."

We would do five of these "Thank You, Hashem's" five times a day.

It was incredibly powerful. For the six months that we consistently focused on this, it pushed us to recognize the positive in our day-to-day lives.

At the end of a day of chemotherapy, we found ourselves thanking God for the wonderful walk we had on Hampstead Heath instead of complaining about the horrors of the disease and its treatment. Even when Elana was dying, this self-training paid off. She might have felt incredibly ill, but her focus was on the fact that she had a husband whom she loved, she had kids to enjoy, she had friends around; she was a Jew and had a relationship with God... There was still so much to be thankful for.

Doing something like this is extremely hard work. It requires a consistent effort to maintain focus. Six months was all we managed on a regular basis. But for those six months, it really changed our lives — and the effects remain with me today, almost five years later.

Morning Blessings

Idea number two is something that I do every single day — and have done for perhaps fifteen years. It's an idea that I heard from Rabbi Weinberg and has proved incredibly meaningful for me.

As always, it takes a bit more time and effort in the beginning, but after that, it is fairly quick. You still only get out as much as you put in, but it's not overly time-consuming.

Initially, it requires an hour, then about fifteen minutes a day for a week and then two minutes a day from then on in.

The initial hour is spent making a list of all the blessings you have in life — all the gifts which you appreciate.

Start with the obvious ones — your arms, your legs, your eyes, your hands, your feet, your mind, your emotions, your parents, your spouse, each one of your children, each one of your siblings... Now move onto some of the blessings that you notice less, but are still of serious value to you. Imagine, for example, life without your fingernails, or without your hair, or without your eyelashes. They are all blessings to appreciate. Each friend is a gift. Your free will is a gift. Wisdom is a gift. Hearing is a gift. Running water is a gift. A roof over your head is a gift. Food is a gift. The ability to love is a gift.

The list, of course, goes on forever, but if you take between half an hour and an hour, you should cover the most significant blessings in your life.

That's the hardest bit done. Now, you take some time over the next week to prioritize your top fifteen gifts. For example, what is more valuable to you, your eyes or your arms? Most people would say their eyes, but that's just because they are not appreciating their arms. Blind people can be very independent. People without arms need someone to go to the bathroom with them every time. Eyes give us vision, but arms give us independence. That's an incredible gift. When you think about it, arms probably mean more to us. But there's no right and wrong. Prioritize in your own way.

Now you have a list of your fifteen greatest blessings in life. All you need to do next is to thank God for every single one of them, every single day, right after you wake up and get dressed in the morning. Don't just say, "Thank You, God, for my eyes" (if eyes are in your top fifteen). Express it in a way that gets you to feel the blessing. Say, "Thank You, God, for my eyes — which mean I can see. I can look at our children today. I can appreciate how beautiful my wife's smile is. I can look at the colors of a flower and the detail of a Rembrandt. I can walk out of my house, knowing where I'm going. I can play sports. I can drive a car. I can read a book... Wow — I am so blessed to have eyes!"

The idea is to enjoy the pleasure and savor it. For my oldest son, for example, I say, "Thank You, God, for Akiva; he is responsible and he cares about his siblings very deeply. He is generous and loving and intelligent. Thank You." I think of him as I say it and try to feel how much he means to me and how appreciative I am of him.

Do the same for all fifteen. It shouldn't take you more than two minutes or so a day — but I guarantee you that over time it will transform your level of happiness during the day.

As I said, I started almost fifteen years ago and do it every single day. On a difficult day, when I wake up in the morning feeling that I just can't face life, I go through my greatest gifts, and it changes my whole perspective. It might not last the whole day (though sometimes it does), but at least it gets me off to a very good start. I did this even when I was sitting shivah for Elana, and it helped a great deal.

The point is that life really is good for every single one of us. It isn't just good, it's overflowing with goodness. But we get so focused on the frustrations of life that we forget the goodness. This exercise is simply to remind us of that which we know and yet forget, pretty much every single day.

When you see that life is good and you feel just how good it is, then when "bad" happens, you are able to put it into perspective much more easily. Painful things don't mean that life is bad. Life is still very good, but you are facing a difficult challenge right now.

I used to say, "Thank You, God, for my beautiful wife Elana." After she passed away, my immediate response was to remove her from my list. But I found a new insight and didn't. Instead, I say, "Thank You, God, for twelve years with a very special woman." If you were to give me the option of never having met Elana and having avoided the pain of losing her — I would not hesitate to decline. The time I spent with her is still one of the fifteeen greatest blessings of my life. I could easily complain that God did not give me more time with her. But doing this will only prevent me from appreciating and enjoying the blessing that she was to me. Even on a simplistic level, why should I choose a feeling of bitterness over a feeling of goodness?

And this is the bottom line for us all. The choice of whether we focus on the good or on the bad is always ours. Focus on the bad and you can be a miserable emperor of the world. Focus on the good and you can be happy when dying of cancer — as Elana always was.

Another Cancer Patient

I once met a cancer patient who was in remission. It was well before my own experiences with Elana.

He came to me after a class in which I was talking about some of the above ideas and told me that he very much related to what I was talking about. He was a cancer patient and had fairly recently been undergoing serious chemotherapy in a hospital in New York City. He said that he had been so sick from the chemo that he couldn't see properly, couldn't hear properly, couldn't walk without feeling dizzy. He was throwing up all the time. He happened to be in a room facing a busy street and was able to look outside and see people hurrying past. Everyone seemed to be in a big hurry to get somewhere, but they didn't look particularly happy. In fact, he felt they actually looked quite miserable.

He said that if he could have, he would have screamed out of the window, "Idiots, why are you so miserable? You can see properly, you can walk without being dizzy. You are not throwing up constantly. You are not battling a terminal illness. You should be skipping. You should be dancing. You should be singing."

He swore to himself that if he ever made it into remission, he would make sure that he danced. And so he did. Not long after, the chemo had done its job and he was released from hospital. He said to me that for two whole weeks, he had sung; he had danced; he had skipped down the street without a care in the world.

"Now, Rabbi," he told me, "I am back to being one of them."

For two or three weeks he had appreciated just how good life was. And then the frustration of day-to-day life took over and he was miserable once again.

Focusing for a short period of time is not so difficult — especially when we have overcome problems or see others with problems and can appreciate just how good we really do have things.

But maintaining that focus is where the challenge really lies. Remembering how good life is every day, not just at times when outside circumstances awaken us to it, is what will dictate whether we live our lives with a sense of joy or not.

Happiness is not a happening. It's a serious, long-term undertaking. It took me weeks and months and years until I saw changes in myself. And it only took days for me to slip back once I wasn't consciously focusing anymore. Maintaining happiness is not an easy task, but it's certainly possible for the person who is willing to work on it. And is there any greater reward for one's efforts than happiness?

There was something I decided for myself, very soon after Elana died. I realized that I could lose my wife and be miserable. Or I could lose my wife and be happy. Losing my wife was something totally beyond my control. In my mind, God had made a good but painful decision for me. But happiness? That was entirely within my own hands. Losing my wife was something painful, but being unhappy would be something even worse. Why have two painful things happen to me when it only needed to be one? Why not take control where I had the opportunity to do so and not allow the second painful thing to compound my misery?

And so I did.

I'm not saying that I was happy every day. But I made a conscious decision that I would not be depressed. It was not artificially fooling myself and suppressing my emotions so that I didn't feel the sadness. It was a genuine focus on all the incredible goodness that I still had, instead of the one deeply painful thing I had lost.

Happiness is first and foremost a decision. And it is a decision that each and every one of us can make if we find the strength to do so.

Chemical imbalance, personality, and circumstances all play a role, to be sure. But none of these even come close to the power of the human will when we make a decision. Decide to be happy and you will be happy — maybe not today, tomorrow, or even in three months. But you will be happy because ultimately happiness is entirely within our own power to choose.

Chapter 7

STRATEGY 3: PRAYER

We Jews believe that prayer has real power. God listens to our prayers and takes them seriously. Prayer can change reality.

Because of that power, prayer can help us avoid the feeling of helplessness that so often accompanies difficult circumstances.

One of the great challenges of an illness like secondary cancer — though it applies to many other circumstances — is the feeling of lack of control. You just don't know what's going on. The doctors don't know what's going on; they don't really know if they can cure you — and if they had to take a guess, they'd probably say they can't. It's all doom and gloom and there is seemingly nothing you can do.

Well, let me tell you that there is very much something you can do. You can pray. And it will empower you significantly, by throwing the ball back into your court. Once you pray, you retake control. You have, through your relationship with the Being who controls all circumstances, the ability to turn things around — the ability to turn anything around.

The more sincerity and commitment you are able to pray with, the more you will feel that you really are doing something. You are not just sitting and watching while something bad happens to you. You are fighting it with a powerful weapon.

Whether or not you end up winning is not what matters. What matters is that you are a fighter in a battle, not a helpless victim. You have a Friend who can help — and an omnipotent Friend, at that.

How one should pray, modes of prayer, and tapping into the power of prayer are issues that are beyond the scope of this particular book, but suffice it to say that prayer is, in and of itself, deeply comforting.

God Is Not a Vending Machine

A number of people asked me how I felt about the fact that I prayed so much for Elana — and I really did — and yet my prayers were not answered. Not only did I pray, but hundreds and thousands of others poured out their hearts for Elana — and yet she died.

I have often heard people say in response to this question that God always answers our prayers, but sometimes His answer is "no." I don't believe this answer. I believe that prayer is much more powerful than that.

God's answer is always a positive answer. But sometimes the answer is positive in the way you asked for it, and sometimes the answer is positive in a way you didn't imagine.

I can't say that I came to this insight easily.

During shivah, I was really struggling to relate to the words we say three times in the morning service, "God is our savior. Our king will answer us on the day that we call" (Psalms 20:10). Well, I had called and called and called for almost three years. I had cried tropical rainstorms of tears — and I had not been answered. My wife had died.

I asked Rabbi Weinberg, my teacher, and he gave me an answer that, after a good amount of thought, felt very right to me. I was asking God to heal my wife. And He did. But not in the way I was looking for. The way He healed her was greater than anything I could have imagined. He healed her not physically, but spiritually, and I was and am envious of the spiritual health that she attained. A few days before she passed away, she said that for the first time in her life, she truly felt that God loved her. She had always known it, but had never been able to fully feel it. Now she did. She felt at one with God and at one with me. She felt at one with herself and she knew that life really is beautiful. While her body was as sick as a body can be, her soul was healthier than anyone I had ever met. Even two days before her passing, she told me that she would not swap places with anyone.

Why couldn't God heal her soul and body, both? It's a good question, but if we knew God's ways — we would be God Himself! I don't know why both were not possible. But I do know that God did heal her. And if for some reason there had to be a choice between spiritual and physical health, I know which she would have chosen — and I also know which I like to think I would have had the strength to choose had our roles been reversed.

God answered when I called — just not with the answer I asked for. But God is not a vending machine. You don't just insert your prayer, push a button, and receive your Pepsi. Rather, God is a loving, caring Father with whom we have a dynamic relationship. We pray. He listens, considers, and decides how best to respond, based on who we are and what we need. And His answer is always positive.

Growth from Prayer

Every prayer I said for my wife changed me. It changed my relationship with her. It changed my relationship with myself, and, of course, it changed my relationship with God. No prayer was wasted. Each accomplished its mission — that of making me a little more Godly. Each prayer softened my heart and humbled me. I am a very different person today because of the intensity of the prayers I said for my wife during her illness.

Judaism maintains that we are here in this world to get closer to God. Through our prayers, Elana got closer to God; I got closer to God; those around us also got closer to God; the thousands who prayed for her got closer to God. The details of the situation were painful, even horrific. It is not the way that any of us wanted it to happen, but the results were those that we were looking for. Our prayers were answered in an incredibly positive way.

We can't expect to understand every aspect of what happens in the world. We don't tell our kids everything, and God doesn't tell us everything, either. But this we can know: we pray and He answers us. We might not always fully understand His answer, but it is always a loving "yes." And we will always be better people because of it.

Bitachon

Trusting in God is probably the key to it all. If you can feel that God is on your side, loving you and doing what is best for you, then you should feel comfortable with any circumstance that comes your way.

Easy to say, Rabbi.

But as I have said before, anything good does not come easy.

As we know, trust in God does not just happen. You don't go

to bed one night feeling that God is out to get you and wake up the next day confident that you can rely on Him — no matter what illegal substances you might be taking.

If you want to trust God, it is going to take conscious effort to develop and maintain the emotion.

So how do you do it?

Let's begin with two prerequisites — feeling trust and having an intellectual foundation for your trust.

1. Feeling Trust

First, trust is a feeling. You can intellectualize all you want, but if you don't, for example, "feel" confident that someone will catch you at the bottom of the ladder, you aren't going to jump.

There's an old story of the atheist who falls off a cliff one thousand feet high. He grabs onto a single twig five hundred feet down. He looks up to Heaven and figures he doesn't have all that many options.

"Is there anybody up there?" he asks.

"Yes, it's Me, God," comes the response.

"Thank God for that," the atheist replies. "Please God, help me. I'll do anything."

"Of course, my son. But I have just one request to make."

"Anything, God," replies the atheist.

"I will save you, my child," says God, "but you have to trust Me first. Let go of the twig and I will catch you."

The atheist looks down at the rocks five hundred feet below and looks up again.

"Is there anybody else up there?"

The point is clear. You can know there's a God intellectually, but that doesn't mean you'll trust Him emotionally. A person can switch from being an atheist to a believer in a single moment — if he or she were to have a clear experience of God. But trusting in God is a very different matter.

2. Knowledge — Not Faith

The second prerequisite is that if you want to trust God, you first have to know He exists and loves you. We human beings have a dangerous ability to feel emotions that are intellectually unsupported and unsupportable. People can, for example, experience "love" for someone who has none of the qualities they are truly looking for. We call it infatuation. Similarly, people can find deep meaning in something that is utterly meaningless. (Suicide bombers feel it incredibly meaningful to take innocent lives.) And people can have faith in something that, intellectually, is clearly false — the Moonies and other cults prey on this constantly.

So too, people can trust in God without being sure that He even exists. As silly as it might sound, it happens quite regularly. It is not only incorrect, but also dangerous. It's dangerous because it's mindless. Wherever there is mindlessness, there is reliance on emotion. And emotions can get us to feel and do things that, given the time to think about, we would never dream of doing.

Trust cannot be a crutch. It must start with the mind and then permeate the emotions. Otherwise, it's a castle built on sand.

I'm going to talk now about how to deepen one's trust in God. If you are confident intellectually in God's existence, working on the following ideas will help you feel a deeper sense of closeness and confidence in him. If, however, your knowledge of God is only on an emotional level, I suggest that you work on gaining real knowledge before contemplating the ideas that I am about to present.

The Seven Elements of Bitachon

According to the tenth century classic, *Chovos HaLevavos* (Duties of the Heart), there are seven elements involved in trust in God (*Shaar HaBitachon*, ch. 2). If you feel all seven, your trust will be complete. But it's not an all-or-nothing proposition. Any level of any of these elements will help you feel some sense of trust. I am not using the order of the original book, but rather, an order put together by Rabbi Weinberg.

Tell yourself that:

1. God loves me with a love that is deeper than the love I have for my children or that my parents have for me. In fact, it is deeper than the love of any parent for any child. In fact, if one combined into a single intense emotion all of the love of every parent for every child since time began, God's love for me would be deeper and more intense. God loves me as a unique individual. I am his special, sweet little baby.

   I personally try to imagine God holding me in His arms, smiling at me, as I do with my children, enveloping me in His love.

2. God knows my every need, my every challenge, and my every problem. He knows what I feel, what I think, what concerns me, what worries me. He knows exactly what's on my mind and He knows it constantly. He doesn't forget about me, not even for a moment. Nothing slips past Him. He "thinks" about me and my problems 24/7.

   During Elana's illness, I thought, *He knows the location of every cancer cell in her body. No rogue cell can slip by unnoticed and start growing on its own. He is fully aware and cognizant of all that is going on. He is in complete control and charge of every single cell of her body and takes no time off.*

He also knows what is worrying me — what's on my mind. He knows my concerns and my fears. He knows my hopes and my aspirations. He knows exactly what I'm feeling, exactly what I want. Whenever I might choose to speak to Him, at any time of day, He is listening and taking me seriously, before I even begin.

3. God has the power to do anything. There is nothing that I need that He cannot provide; nothing I am lacking that is not His to give. He is able to solve all my problems and solve them immediately. He is not only able to solve current problems; he is fully capable of preventing any new problems from arising.

   In the context of Elana, I was always sure that He had the ability to take away every single cancer cell instantly. I would think, *He can change the whole situation around in a moment. And it's not difficult for Him to do so. My wife could jump out of bed tomorrow, free of cancer, as though nothing had ever happened. Whether or not He will do that is another issue. But He certainly CAN do so.*

4. Nothing else has any power. There is nothing that works independent of God. Nothing, no matter how small, can or does happen without His full approval and intimate involvement. He does not give His power to other forces. He remains in full control at all times.

   There is no cancer; there is just God. There is no chemotherapy; there is just God. Cancer cells do not grow by themselves; God makes them grow. And there is not a single one that can grow without God's command for it to do so. God and cancer are not adversaries. They are partners. No treatment can circumvent His will. If He wishes the treatment to work, then it will, and if He does not, then it will not.

5. God has done so much for me until now. He has given me life. He has given me free will. He makes my heart beat. He makes the blood run through my body. He gives me air to

breathe, food to eat. He provides warmth. He has given me intelligence, emotions, time in this world, eyes, legs, arms, ears... You name it, He has done it. He has a track record of complete and utter unwarranted goodness to me. Given how He has related to me up to now, surely anything I need or want is a small thing in comparison.

It's like asking my father for a dime to make a phone call. It's a small-time request compared to what he has already done. If he did not give it to me, I would be absolutely shocked.

Taking the cancer away is nothing compared to making my heart constantly pump just enough oxygen to my brain for the past thirty-five years. And He did that without my even asking. Surely, if I ask Him, He will take my prayer very seriously.

6. God's love is unconditional. It is not dependent on my actions or my way of life. Like a good parent, He loves me no matter what. Even when I stumble and make some very big mistakes, He still loves me. Even when I completely ignore Him, He loves me. His love is with me no matter who I am or what I do. Despite all my imperfections, I can feel secure that God is still backing me.

   Yes, God would like me to be great. Yes, His expectations for me are massive — because of what I can accomplish with the soul He has given me. But those expectations are purely based on His desire to give to me. He expects because He wants me to find fulfillment. And so, I could waste all my potential and He might still make Elana better, just because He loves me. And if He did not, it would only be that because of His love for me, He knows that this is what is best for me.

7. Like any good parent, God will always give me just what I need. Life will not always be exactly what I want to it be. He may not give me what I think will be good for me. But He will

always give me what is really good for me. No matter what I am going through, it is exactly what I need to be going through.

Whatever God might have in store for me, the road this illness is taking us down is a road we need to traverse. And wherever that road might lead, its destination is where we need to get to.

For me, this final point creates the greatest sense of trust and security. No matter what I am going through — no matter how "bad" or painful it may seem, I know that it is for my ultimate good.

During the difficult months after my wife's passing, this point was always one that I could fall back on. God gives me what I need. This is what I need. It is not bad. It is good. It will bring me closer to Him — if I choose for it to do so.

Try feeling each of these elements a number of times a day. Elana and I used to do it ten times a day at regular intervals. We found doing it together fun, as we would alternate the elements and try to get each other to really feel each one. If you do it on your own, I suggest you don't spend too much time on each one, as it can be frustrating. Taking just one minute to focus on all of these points a few times a day will make a significant impact.

It won't happen overnight. You need to be patient. It is my belief that Torah works. The Rabbis know what they are talking about. There is amazing wisdom in Rabbeinu Bachya's *Chovos HaLevavos*. Yet it does require patience. It took a number of months before I began to see a lasting effect from doing this. But that's Judaism. If you want instant results, I'm afraid you'll have to find yourself a different religion.

Working on feeling these seven elements for developing trust has been very powerful for me. It has brought a tremendous sense of security into my life. Spending a few minutes a day is a small price to pay for the eternal dividends that you can reap.

Chapter 8

Strategy 4: It's All for the Best

The Rabbis tell us that whenever anything that seems bad happens to you, you should say, "*Gam zu letovah* — this too, is for the best." They tell the story of Rabbi Akiva who had a donkey, a candle, and a rooster (*Berachos* 60b). He went into a city to find a place to sleep and was turned away. "*Gam zu letovah*," he said and went to spend the night in a field outside the city. His lamp blew out in the wind. *Gam zu letovah* once again. Then his rooster and his donkey both died. Also *gam zu letovah*.

When he awoke in the morning, he ventured into the city and realized that bandits had attacked it during the night, killing many people. Had he found a place to stay, he would probably have been killed. Had the bandits noticed a lamp in a field nearby or heard his donkey or rooster, he might also have been in trouble. Instead, his life was saved by all the "bad" things that happened to him.

There is an important note that must go with this story. If God had wanted to save Rabbi Akiva from the bandits, surely He could have let him find a nice room in the city for himself, his lamp, his rooster, and his donkey and let him sleep through the night unmolested. If God is all powerful, then He can do things in a way that is more, rather than less, comfortable. Rabbi Akiva might have been saved, but he still went through pain. Why could he not have been saved in a painless way?

I think that there was a message here for Rabbi Akiva. Yes, he was a great enough man that he should be saved in a miraculous way. But he did not merit an open miracle of staying in the city and being saved during a rampage. There was something lacking in him that God was trying to point out to him. Yes, it was good — for it is always good. But it was painful also, and in pain there is always a lesson.

In the *Amidah* that we say every day of the year, it states that God is *gomel chasadim tovim* — He does good deeds of kindness. This seems, at first glance, to be redundant. Surely deeds of kindness are all "good." How could a kindness be bad?

The answer is that you can be kind and nice to someone — but that is not necessarily what is best for them. People will sometimes benefit more from painful experiences than nice ones. Unless it is our children, this is not for us to decide. We need to be nice, give people pleasant experiences and leave the painful ones for God to mete out.

There is still, however, a question. The *Amidah* says that God is a doer of "good kindnesses." This does not seem to be correct. Almost every day in almost every person's life, there will be goodness that does not feel so kind. Goodness is unarguable — for we do not see a complete picture — but whether a circumstance feels good to us or not is something we can certainly judge. And very often it does not. So how can we say that God does "good kindnesses"?

I think the answer lies in the context of the phrase. This is in the *Amidah* — we are praising God in prayer. We are talking about who God is in real terms; what He is in essence. In essence, God is a Being who does "good kindnesses." That is His nature, so to speak. But in the reality of this world, He is not always able to do that. He has given us free will, and if He is to maintain that, He must sometimes respond to our decisions with pain. It hurts Him, so to speak, much more than it hurts us. But it is what He needs to do. It is not the way He would choose to act, but given the greater good of free will, it is the way that He must act.

So we are told to say "*gam zu letovah*" immediately upon something "bad" happening to us.

When we first heard of Elana's cancer, I found it very difficult to say this to myself. In fact, Elana was able to say it much sooner than I was and she only gradually was able to help me say it also.

The whole experience caused me to examine what the Rabbis mean by giving us this phrase, and I discovered an insight that has made it possible for me to say it very easily nowadays.

I used to understand the idea as follows. When something bad happens to you, take a moment to remind yourself that God has a plan; that He knows what He's doing and He's not making a mistake. It looks bad, but that's only how it looks on the surface. You'll look back one day and realize just how good it was.

That's how I used to understand the purpose of saying this phrase — simply to remind us that God is in control at a time that one might panic and forget.

Now I think that the psychology of this idea is much, much deeper.

We live in a world of good and bad. In fact, almost every aspect of this world is neither wholly good nor wholly bad, but a fusion of both. There is little, if anything, that is black or white. Everything is gray. Even something like Torah — a book of wisdom for life — the Rabbis tell us can be an elixir of life or an elixir of death. There is good and bad. People are the same. Every single human being has his good traits and bad traits.

The same is true of events in our lives. Our response is that which defines which way they will go, whether an event is something that will naturally bring more good feeling to our lives or naturally bring us more problems.

All events, as such, are a mixture of potential good and potential bad.

You win the lottery. There is a lot of good there. You can support your family. You can enjoy God's beautiful world. You can give money to charity. You can be free to pursue meaning and wisdom. That's all great. But with money comes other things.

From now on, how will you know who is sincere in their friendship for you? How will you be able to trust people? You will become much more of a target for robbery. You will be much more likely to worry and think about losing your money now that you have it. I remember once talking to a man who lives in a forty-million-dollar house on a beautiful road in London. He was telling me about how wonderful his security was — he had dogs and he had cameras throughout his house, as well as all the way up his driveway. (Before the cameras, he was once attacked in his driveway and he and his wife were beaten up before the thieves ran off with his money.) I told him that I have no cameras. I have no dogs. I open my door to strangers without fear. Is the money really worth it? And he wasn't sure.

Money has its blessings but also its curses. It's just that the blessings are more immediately obvious and the curses are a little more subtle.

The same is true of "bad" things. Let's take a person's house burning down. It's easy to see the bad elements of that, but what about the good? Well, there are many possibilities. Maybe it will give him more humility — something worth much more than a mere house. Maybe he will have to spend time with his family in less spacious surroundings and will have the opportunity to get closer to them as a result. Or maybe even just the challenge itself will be something that brings them closer together. Maybe it will put life and possessions into perspective for him. There are many positive elements one could focus on, depending on the circumstances.

Now, the question arises — when something "bad" like this happens, which is it easier to focus on, the good or the "bad"? Which jumps out at you more? What are you more likely to say when your house burns down — that it's good, or that it's bad?

Obviously, you'd say that it's "bad." The reason is that the pain is so immediate, so real, that it presses itself into your face and screams at you that this is "bad." You will need no help and no encouragement to be able to see the "bad" parts of life's challenges.

What we do, however, need some help with is to balance this out with the good.

Because we need no help with the good, but we do with the bad, the rabbis gave us this phrase to say. As soon as something bad happens, we say, "This, too, is for the good." If you try to be "objective," you will usually come down on the side of bad. Because it's an unfair fight. But you must decide from the very beginning that this is good. You tell yourself, you push yourself, you make a definite and absolute decision — the fact that my house burned down is good. Now you are approaching the issue from a totally different perspective. Instead of saying, "Let me see if there is good in this also," you say, "Let me see where the good is."

And when you are looking for it, you will invariably find it — because it exists in every circumstance in life.

Tell yourself that it is good — and you will go and find out why. Tell yourself that you're not sure — and you will, almost certainly, see it as bad. You have to fight to see the good, and a conviction of that good will give you the strength to do so.

Saying "*gam zu letovah*" (and meaning it) is an incredibly powerful tool. I find that when I do it properly, instead of just going through the motions, I come at an issue with a totally different perspective — a much healthier perspective.

The story is told of the great sage of two thousand years ago, Hillel the Elder. He was walking into his town and heard a great commotion coming from one of the houses. People were screaming and crying and clearly something terrible had happened. He could not hear where the cries were coming from, but he said he could be certain they were not coming from his own house. It is usually understood to mean that Hillel knew that God would not allow something bad like this to happen in his home.

The Shelah (*Asarah Maamaros*, 5) asks a question, however. We know that no one is perfect. Even Hillel made mistakes in his life. How could he be so sure that God would not do something in order to get a message across to him? And even if he could be sure, Hillel is known in the Talmud for his great humility. This does not sound overly humble — to suggest that he was so righteous that nothing could happen to him or his household.

He answers as follows: There was no question in Hillel's mind that painful experiences could happen in his home. But what he knew was that if something did, his household would not respond this way. He was a man versed in the art of "*gam zu letovah*." He lived his life focusing on the good. And he knew that it had rubbed off on the members of his household. In the same way as he would not shout and cry, no matter what happened, he was confident that they would act in the same manner. When "bad" happened, they would surely not scream and wail. They would say "*gam zu letovah*" and start finding the good.

Screaming and wailing could not come from his household. So he could be sure that whatever had happened had not been in his home.

When you say "*gam zu letovah*" and say it again and again and again, you will start to find the good. And the more times you find the good, the more you will become a person who responds with a positive outlook to any painful experience.

Chapter 9

SHIVAH

At the shivah, people came from all over. The house was packed from morning to night with neighbors, friends, family, local *rabbanim*... It was summer vacation time, but people returned from places they had gone to in England and also came from Israel and America.

Elana's presence was strongly felt throughout the week, and I printed up papers of Elana's favorite quote to distribute. They said the following:

> This was Elana's favorite quote. She would like you to think about how to apply it to yourself.
>
>> Our deepest fear is not that we are inadequate. Our deepest fear is that we are powerful beyond measure. It is our light, not our darkness that most frightens us. We ask ourselves, "Who am I to be brilliant, gorgeous, talented, fabulous…?"
>>
>> Actually, who are you not to be?
>>
>> You are a child of God. Your playing small doesn't serve the world. There's nothing enlightened about shrinking so

> that people won't feel insecure around you. We are meant to shine, as children do. We were born to make manifest the glory of God that is within us. It's not just in some of us; it's in everyone. And as we let our own light shine, we unconsciously give other people permission to do the same. As we are liberated from our own fear, our presence automatically liberates others.
>
> From *A Return to Love*, by Marianne Williamson

I also put out a large notebook so that friends and family could record their feelings (see excerpts in the appendix). To this day I read through it and find comfort. It was also important that I have it for our children. None of them knew Elana well enough. None of them were able to truly appreciate what a special mother they had. I wanted something that would help them to do so at a time when they were ready. That time has not come yet for any of them, but I look forward to four special opportunities of sharing it.

The Shabbos of the shivah was quite amazing. No mourning is allowed on Shabbos and I was determined to keep that halachah. In spite of the deep and heavy sorrow hanging over us (it was only two days since she had passed away), I told the kids that we were going to have a good Shabbos. Shabbos is a day to feel oneness with God and, by doing so, to transcend feelings of grief.

And that's exactly what we did. It was a wonderful, spiritual day that we didn't want to end. It wasn't so much an escape from mourning as it was a different perspective on mourning. If there is a God who loves you and you can feel His presence in your life, then other things — even something as tragic as losing someone you love deeply — are placed in perspective.

On Friday night, I was not sure whether to sing *Eishes Chayil* or not. I had always sung it specifically to Elana. Looking at each other as I sang was probably the highlight of our week. How could I possibly sing it with an empty seat opposite me? I didn't think I'd be able to stop myself from crying, and on Shabbos this wasn't the right thing to do.

In the end, I came up with a great idea. I closed my eyes and sang *Eishes Chayil* with a different focus. I thought of it as referring to the Jewish people in their relationship with God. I was singing a beautiful song about the greatness of the Jewish people. Once again, I found myself able to transcend the feeling of pain and was lifted into the realm of the spiritual.

I am not a superman. I didn't want to cry on Shabbos because halachah forbids it. But if I had, I would not have gotten down on myself. We're human and pain is real. I was ready to fail as long as I had made an effort.

During the week of shivah, I felt so detached and lost. I searched desperately for some feeling of connection to Elana. I would go out into the garden and try to feel her presence in the wind, in the trees, in the birds' song — but I could not connect. The house was completely full of people — and at the same time it was completely empty.

She was very much within me, but somehow, I wanted a concrete sign of her presence. I was so hungry for some sort of connection that I even checked her e-mails to see if anything had come in recently. I thought that perhaps I might find something from someone to her that would reconnect me to who she was. She did her e-mails via a phone that sent e-mails as well as text messages, so I opened up her account and logged on.

There were no e-mails. But, strangely, there was one text message still in her Outbox. For some reason, she had never sent it. I saw that it was to be sent to my phone number. I was shaking as I opened it. Three short words, the last words Elana would ever convey to me. It simply said, "I love you."

I had found what I was looking for. Elana, once again, had thought of me to the very last.

Chapter 10

REMARRIAGE

I had thought to conclude the book at this point. However, my editor suggested a chapter on rebuilding the family once Elana had passed away.

Marrying a second time is always difficult. Marrying after going through the intense relationship that I went through with Elana during her last few weeks was surely impossible.

At the same time, I knew that I still had so much to give to a marriage — if anything I felt I had more to give after what I had been through. And I knew also that our children desperately needed a mother.

There are so many challenges that one faces in a situation like this — not least of all a new wife trying to fill the shoes of someone who was so respected, so loved, and so cherished.

I know of cases in which a second wife comes into a situation like this with incredibly good intentions and is undermined by family and friends and anyone who felt close to the first wife. A misguided sense of loyalty seems to make people feel that they must defend the position of the first wife from an opportunist impostor. I must say from the outset that this was not my experience. While people might have had their reservations in advance, mainly because of her age, once I married Chana everyone was incredibly supportive of her and respected the new role that she had courageously undertaken.

But unfortunately, it doesn't always work that way, and I hope that sharing my own experience will help others understand how things can actually work.

Every day, without exception, I thank God for Elana. And every day, without exception, I also thank God for Chana. I feel doubly blessed to have been given two such special women with whom to share different periods of my life.

While the process leading up to my marrying Elana felt almost akin to a fairy tale, the process leading up to marrying Chana was rockier, more painful, and more real — but no less special in its own way.

Chana with Akiva and Sora in Eilat about two months after Elana passed away.

Chana came to help with our children eight months before Elana passed away. At the time, she was eighteen years old. She is number six of twelve children and was very used to taking responsibility for kids. As far as she was concerned, she was coming for a short time to help with a family whose mother was sick. She thought she would stay a little while, the mother would get better, and she would leave. She wasn't quite prepared for what was about to happen to her.

As Chana was a young woman in my house, I steered very clear of her, but her relationship with Elana blossomed. During those eight months, Chana and Elana became incredibly close. Elana trusted Chana implicitly with the children and shared with her many of her values and dreams in child rearing. Chana learned from Elana, grew from Elana, and came to love Elana very deeply. In the short period of time that they knew each other, they developed a very special relationship. When she was really not well, Chana was the one she called in to ask how I was doing and to make sure I had what I needed. She wanted to set Chana up with her brother, but as usual, God had other and always better plans.

After Elana passed away, Chana was the woman the children initially turned to for their emotional needs. But I didn't think it was right of me to place such a burden on an eighteen-year-old girl. I asked her if she wanted to leave, even encouraged her to do so, but she didn't feel that she could abandon the children when they needed her. She was a young woman with so many opportunities, but for her the children, even though they were not her own, came first. To be sure, there were those who questioned her motives — as is to be expected in a situation like this — but time and events would prove just how sincere she was.

A few months after Elana passed away, I started to think about getting married again. It was soon, but I had four young children and I knew that I could not give them all that they needed. I thought about Chana, about her relationship with the kids and with Elana. I remember taking a walk with my eldest daughter, who was eight at the time, and discussing the concept of my getting married again. She had a picture of a "wicked stepmother" and was terrified at the thought. I asked her if there was anyone whom she would be happy with. I went through a list of people she knew and felt close to and each one got a very clear no. I saved Chana for last and ask her what she thought. "Yes, Abba. Please marry Chana," was her immediate answer. (She has since told me that she would never have said that if she knew Chana would cut back on the sweets once we got married!)

It was a painful decision for me, but after much thought I decided that Chana was too young. There was a sixteen year age difference between us. She deserved a young man with no baggage — someone who would cherish her and be excited by her without another woman in the back of his mind. I felt it was selfish and unfair of me even to consider her. Even if she was interested, I believed it was only because she was caught up in the emotions of the situation. I was convinced that if she married me, she would regret doing so at a later date.

Despite the fact that Elana's sister had stayed on to give the children support, we were a single man and single woman caring for the same children in the same house, and it was not a good situation. I knew that the only fair and sensible course of action was for me to insist that she leave. It was painful for me, painful for her, and even more painful for the kids, but in the long run, I honestly believed I was making the right decision for the family.

And so, one year after her arrival and four months after Elana's passing, Chana left for America.

The kids missed her. I missed her much more than I thought I would. But I knew we would get over it. It was time to buckle down to some serious dating.

Given how my relationship had developed with Elana, dating wasn't really something I had done before. I found myself struggling not to cry on certain dates. How could I marry someone who was not Elana? I felt so confused and lost with the whole process. Should I look for someone in the same circumstances as myself? But that would mean double the baggage. I'd heard of marriages that fell apart because the children didn't get along with each other. Or should I look for someone who had never married before? But how would they even begin to relate to what I had been through?

I told myself that at the very least, I needed someone totally different from Elana. I wanted someone who excelled in areas that Elana hadn't. That was the only way I might save myself from constant comparisons. Other than that, I had no idea what I was looking for. Nothing that wasn't Elana made sense to me.

Dating was an incredibly distressing and challenging experience — and it required a liberal use of all the tools I have written about just to keep myself sane, let alone happy and motivated. I knew that things would get better. I knew that the pain would pass and I would again experience incredible goodness in my life. I knew that Hashem had wonderful plans and that this was a piece of the jigsaw puzzle and one day I would see how perfectly it fitted. But it's one thing to know these things and another to be able actually to live with them. During Elana's final illness, I had had Elana there to help me focus properly. Now I was on my own and I wasn't coping as well.

I went through a number of difficult experiences, including a very painful broken engagement; but in the end, I just couldn't hide from the way I felt about Chana. She had supported me and our children in our hour of greatest need. She cared deeply about my family. She loved Elana. I knew that she had an understanding of what marrying a man in my situation would mean for her and the sacrifices she would have to make — and I was confident that she was ready and willing to make those sacrifices.

As had happened with Elana, it didn't take all that long. After a few conversations on the phone, we both knew it was right and we would be getting married. Everything seemed to fall into place. It seemed clear once again just how perfectly God was running His world. The jigsaw pieces were starting to make a lot more sense.

I didn't want to get engaged over the phone, so Chana came to England for a day. For the first time in a long time, I felt a sense of hope. As with Elana, when I proposed and when Chana said yes, my world seemed to take on a whole new level of color and excitement.

When I told the kids, they were excited, but in light of my broken engagement a little skeptical. "Are you really going to do it this time, Abba?" was their response. "We'll believe it when we see it."

As the wedding drew near the kids and I were so excited. But the night before, there was still one issue to deal with. What would the kids call Chana? Of course, they all knew her extremely well by the name Chana. But once we were married, this just wouldn't be right. "Ima" was the name they had called Elana and was clearly not appropriate. "Mum" was completely alien to Chana, since she had been brought up in Israel. We were all a bit stuck. I sat with the four kids on the floor of our hotel room in Jerusalem and we discussed ideas. Auntie Chana — doesn't quite fit. Ima — no good. Mummy — no way!! The kids came up with quite a few funnies. We considered "Wicked Stepmother" for a while, but it was rejected because it was a bit too long. We thought maybe just "Wicked" for short, but we weren't sure that Chana would like it.

"Step" or "Steppy" were rejected by me, even though the kids liked them the best.

After almost an hour, when we were starting to despair, Shifra, my eldest daughter, hit upon the perfect name. "How about 'Mima'?" she said. It wasn't Mum, but it wasn't Ima either. It was a composite that gave the sense of Chana being Ima without explicitly stating it. The moment Shifra said it, we all knew it was right. There was really no discussion about it because we all knew just how perfect it was. Elana will always be Ima for them and have a very special place in their hearts. But their new Mima would be Chana and she would be the one to give them the love they needed from here on in.

I had always wanted a Jerusalem wedding and was disappointed when Elana and I got married in America. It wasn't the way I would have chosen for it to happen, but now God granted me my wish.

I cry at most weddings, but in Jerusalem, I cry at every wedding. When I hear the words, "*Od yishama b'arei Yehudah u'vechutzos Yerushalayim* — Once again will be heard in the hills of Judah and the courtyards of Jerusalem, the sound of joy and the sound of happiness, the sound of a groom and the sound of a bride," I always feel a swelling of emotion. I visualize the prophet Jeremiah standing on a hillside looking down as the Jews leave Israel in chains for Babylon. I imagine him with tears streaming down his face. He would be justified to feel deep despair, but instead he prophesies a prophecy of hope — a prophecy that once again there will be happiness in Jerusalem, there will be weddings and celebrations. I think of Jeremiah and then I think of the wedding I am at. Here I am in direct fulfillment of his 2,500-year-old prophecy. I am standing in Jerusalem witnessing a wedding — exactly as he had said Jews would. How fortunate is our generation to see it come true, to see his dream fulfilled. We are the ones he was talking of... Like I say, I cannot help but cry.

And now it would be my own wedding.

On the day of the wedding I visited Elana's grave on Har HaMenuchos. I knew that she would approve. I knew how she felt about Chana and I knew that she would want me to be happy and the children to have a mother who loved them. It was an emotional experience for me, but I felt at one with her.

For Chana, this wedding was not just for me and her. It was also for "our" children. She made an incredible effort to be sure that they had new clothes for the wedding, that the girls had their hair done in a fancy style, that they were taken care of and looked after at every point. She found friends to care for them before, during, and after the wedding. While I would have been happy to forget about them for the week of *sheva berachos* and focus on our relationship instead, Chana insisted that we be in touch regularly. So many people remarked to me how beautiful it was to see Chana

Chana and I on our wedding day in 2002.

dancing with my daughters and sitting with them on her lap in the bridal chair. She was a twenty-year-old bride. This was her special day. But her concern lay with making sure the children were happy. It was a truly special occasion that one had to witness to fully appreciate.

Once again, our wedding video shows me taking tissue after tissue as I cry under the *chuppah*. Yes, I cried at the thought that now I was not just watching, but actually taking part in the fulfillment of Jeremiah's prophecy. But I also cried in deep happiness and gratitude — exactly as I had the first time around. I was marrying a very special *bas Yisrael*; a girl who was ready to risk marrying someone who still loved someone else; a girl who more than anything wanted to give our children a stable, warm, and loving home; a girl whom I felt would never replace Elana, but who would feel as strongly about me as Elana had and whom I could feel as strongly about as I had about Elana. A girl who Elana had loved and who had loved Elana, too. I felt that Hashem had found the perfect situation for me and I was overwhelmed by His goodness. I was looking forward to our marriage with great hope. As I write this book, two and a half years (and two more children) later, all of those hopes have been fulfilled.

I spoke to someone about marrying again not long after Elana died. He had been through what I had been through ten years earlier and had remarried a year after his wife passed away. I asked if he had found the same happiness in his second marriage as he had in his first. Not the same, he had responded. Different, but equal.

That is how I feel about Chana. She is not Elana. But I don't need her to be Elana. I need her to be Chana. And as Chana, I appreciate her for who she is in the way that I appreciated Elana for who she was. There is no comparison. I don't believe I felt more strongly about either. Just differently. And I believe that in a different way I am as happy with Chana as I was with Elana.

In bringing up the children, Chana is a student of Elana. Like I said, Elana taught Chana an incredible amount about being a mother and Chana always feels that she wants to bring up the children the way that Elana would have. She remembers Elana well, thinks of her often, talks to the children regularly about her, and feels no sense of insecurity about her.

When Chana came into the house, I made sure all the pictures of Elana had been taken down and put away. Gradually, one by one, Chana put them back. She wants our children to cherish the memory of their Ima and knows that pictures play an important role.

Never once, even in times of frustration, have I heard Chana refer to any of the kids as "your children." They are always "our children." We have since been blessed with two more children and Chana relates to them no differently than to the other four. For her, she has six children who are all equal in her eyes.

Chana doesn't like me to thank her, so I won't. But I know it's

Chana and I on vacation in the Alps.

not easy for her to have taken on all that she has taken on at a young age. She has six children and has filled the shoes of a deeply respected, loved, and admired woman. Her greatest challenge of all, however, is the one she enjoys the most — and that is being married to me!

The Children

People would often ask me how the kids were doing after Elana had passed away. My standard answer was, "Ask me in twenty years." Who is to say what deep feelings may remain dormant? I am not a prophet. To the best of my perception, however, I see them as well adjusted, normal, happy kids who miss their Ima, but don't allow that to undermine their lives.

There are principally two methods of dealing with children during times of stress and sorrow. There are those who would protect them from knowing what is going on, and there are those who would keep them informed.

Elana and I strongly believed in the latter. Information — but information given with optimism and confidence — was our policy. We figured that children are more scared of the unknown than they are of the known. At least if they heard from us, and we were open about it from day one, they would not be afraid to ask questions and share their feelings. And this ended up being the case. Throughout Elana's illness, none of our children held back from talking to us whenever they needed to. And since her passing, they have also been open with their feelings. I believe that this policy of honesty has deeply enhanced their sense of security.

It's interesting to see the way a child's mind works. Our son Elkana had just turned five when Elana passed away. I remember that, a few weeks after her passing, he suddenly said to me with great excitement, "Now you can buy a motorbike!"

"Why is that, Elkana?" I questioned, not getting his point.

"Because Ima is dead!" was his eager response.

I realized that he had once overheard a conversation between me and Elana. I had said how much I would love to get a motorbike to navigate through London traffic, and Elana had absolutely forbidden it. Now that she was not around, he reasoned very sensibly, I had nothing to stop me!

About three weeks after Elana passed away, I took the kids to Switzerland to try to get away from it all.

Chana came, as well as Elana's sister, Shira, and a friend of mine from America, whom the kids refer to as Uncle Yitz. We rented a van in Zurich and drove to St. Moritz. Uncle Yitz suggested that I drive first and I was happy to do so, to keep my mind occupied. I had my suspicions that Uncle Yitz had no intent of driving at all.

Soon we were heading up very windy mountain roads, and at every turn there was a barrier protecting us from a massive drop. I was in the driver's seat and Uncle Yitz was in the passenger seat with my daughter, Shifra, in between us. Shifra was deep in

The children at Elana's graveside at the sheloshim.

thought and suddenly asked me what would happen if the car went over the edge of the cliff.

Never one to pull punches with the kids, I told her that of the eight people in the van, probably two would die immediately, one would be critically injured, two would be seriously injured, and two would be moderately injured.

Shifra went quiet for a while and so did I. I was thinking of Elana. After a few minutes she said to me, "Abba, if the car goes off the cliff, I think I want to be one of the people who dies."

"Why is that, Shifra?" I asked, already knowing her answer, for I was thinking the exact same thing.

"That way I can be with Ima," she responded.

I nodded and said back to her, "I think I'd also like to be one of those who die."

Uncle Yitz looked over at both of us and said, "Okay! I think it's time for me to drive!"

Elkana, the five-year-old, was the one who spoke the least about Elana's passing and finally, a few months later, I decided the time had come to try to draw him out. I asked him if he was sad that his Ima had died.

"No," was his immediate response — and to a great extent this was true. He is not the type to dwell on the past. Of all our children he is the one who is the most happy-go-lucky.

At any rate, I thought I would try a different tack to get some sort of response from him. "I feel very sad that Ima died and I miss her a lot," I said.

Again, he responded straight away, "Don't worry, Abba. You can always watch her in the family videos!"

At that point, I conceded defeat.

Although Akiva probably had the hardest time and felt Elana's passing the most acutely, he is now the most well-adjusted of all the children, and I don't believe that to be a coincidence. Children, like adults, need to be able to express and experience their pain. Pain that is held in, or even unacknowledged consciously, lasts a great deal longer than pain that is allowed to express itself.

Recently, Chana had the flu and Akiva said to her, "Oh, no! Not another sick mother! We've already been in the sick mother business!"

Sora Rosa never really knew her Ima. She was only three-and-a-

All six of our children.

half when Elana passed away. She understood that Ima went to be with Hashem and that one day we would all see Ima again, but it might take a long time. But it's not easy to explain to a three-year-old what death means. Some of my darkest moments were when I heard her calling for her Ima in the middle of the night.

I look back on all of these times and think of what a roller-coaster ride it has been. It's been difficult. It's been challenging. But I believe that we went together, as a family, through a long and dark tunnel — and came out on the other side into a bright and gorgeous day. Who knows what Hashem has in store for our future? Whatever it may be, it will only be good.

Conclusion

The title of this book is *Finding Light in the Darkness*, and that is precisely the point I hope I have made.

We live in a world of pain and there is absolutely nothing we can do to circumvent that reality. We can hide from pain, we can experience pain with or without dignity, or we can appreciate that pain is one of God's greatest and most versatile gifts to humanity. It allows us to make meaningful choices about how we want to live our lives. It offers us the opportunity of independence. It shakes us out of apathy and into reality. And it pushes us to achieve and accomplish in a way that we otherwise never would.

In fact, just about the only downside of pain is that it hurts. But even that downside is limited inasmuch as the hurt is always only temporary.

As a society, we need to afford pain its rightful place. Running from it, as we often do, is not a path that will lead to happiness. We certainly don't go looking for pain, but when it comes, let's try to learn to treat it as a friend. I hope that the ideas and exercises contained within this book will contribute to your doing so. Elana left me with many gifts, but this was her greatest. It is to her that I give credit for all I have written — may her memory be blessed.

Appendix A

ELANA'S WORDS

Elana Rosenblatt passed away in London on August 8, 2001. In her thirty short years, she accomplished more than many do in twice or three times that amount of time. Always smiling, always giving, always thinking about others — never about herself. Even in her final illness, when she was weak and in great distress, she was always positive, confident in God's love for her, whatever may be. This article is based on classes she gave about a year before she passed away.

Isn't Life Beautiful?

BY ELANA ROSENBLATT

When I first felt the lump, I was sure that it had everything to do with nursing my six-month-old baby, and nothing at all to do with cancer.

I live in England and I was soon going to America to see my parents, so I pushed it to the back of my mind. When I returned home, I could tell the lump had gotten bigger. It was time to see the doctor.

"Don't worry," he said. "Come back in two weeks — if it's still there."

It was still there. And it was close to Rosh HaShanah. The doctor said, "I'm sure it's nothing, but I want you to have a clear mind for the holidays, so I'm sending you to a surgeon for an evaluation."

I went to the surgeon, who sent me for a mammogram and a biopsy — again, just to be sure it was nothing. Nobody wanted to believe that a twenty-seven-year-old new mother could have breast cancer.

A few days before Yom Kippur we returned to the surgeon. We sat in his waiting room for what seemed like an eternity. Finally, we were called in.

He looked at me and said, "It's cancer." It was like a fist in my gut.

Yet life continued. That day it was my turn to do carpool, so my husband and I went straight from the surgeon's office to my daughter's school. We were quite late, and my carpool kids were all waiting in the headmistress's room.

As I went in, I figured the headmistress was going to have to know sooner or later; I might as well tell her now. When she heard my news, I saw such love and care in her eyes. She said, "Anything you need, we're here for you." She was someone I hardly knew, as it was my daughter's first year in the school, but the love that I felt from her was absolute. This was my first taste of so many loving acts to follow from friends and strangers alike.

We got home, and I dropped the kids off at unsuspecting neighbors. Now my husband and I had a chance to talk.

It was a very emotional time, and we both had a lot we needed to say, but there was one idea that repeatedly came up: God does not do anything that is not perfect.

Life is a puzzle. As we add the pieces of the puzzle one by one, the picture becomes clearer. Sometimes we're not sure where to put a piece; we can't even imagine how it's going to fit. We hold it up and turn it over in our hand and we feel sure that someone must have made a mistake — surely this piece does not belong to this puzzle.

There is no mistake. This piece belongs. As we put together this jigsaw puzzle of our lives, the pieces fit together so beautifully that the seams between them seem to disappear and an awesome picture emerges.

Two hours before I lit Yom Kippur candles, we got a phone call. At first the doctor had been only 99 percent sure the cancer was metastatic. Now she was 100 percent sure.

I was able to see this call as a blessing, too. After all, I had found this out before Yom Kippur and still had the opportunity of this holy day before me. This is the day God is closest to us, the day on which we have the most special relationship with Him. I felt that my fate was not yet sealed.

Sukkos came four days later. We left our sturdy home and went out to live in a flimsy sukkah. The sukkah, with its rickety walls and roof of branches that doesn't protect us from the elements, teaches us that our protection comes from Heaven, not from anything in the physical world. With these thoughts in mind, I started chemotherapy.

As time went on, the jigsaw was making more and more sense. But there are always pieces that don't fit straight away.

Nietzsche said that man can deal with any "what" as long as he has a good enough "why." Let's say you're working out to get in shape. Your muscles are killing you. You're stretching to the breaking point. But you persevere — because it means enough to you. It's painful, but it's worth it. The "why" overcomes the "what."

This is pain that you choose. What about when the pain comes from outside of you? Picture a runner training for the Olympics. The trainer has him running thirty miles a day. He also has to be up very early, keep to a very strict diet, and lift weights for hours. You look at this and think, *Why is the trainer putting him through so much torture?* But the trainer's not putting him through torture; the trainer knows he has the potential to win. And he wants to bring that potential into reality.

When I go for chemotherapy and it takes them six tries to find a vein, not one of those times was unnecessary. Each jab was exactly perfect for what I need. There are no accidents.

Worry, not pain, is my enemy.

There are two things I do to strengthen myself:

First, I make a list of worries that never came true — all the things I worried over that never actually materialized, leaving me with only the hours I had wasted.

Second, several times a day I go over different aspects of the special relationship I have with God. I do this to stay one step ahead of the doubt. And one step ahead of the fear.

Prayer is part of this relationship. Will my prayers be answered the way I want them answered? This I can't know. But I believe that if I ask for God's help, the outcome is more likely to be something easier to accept as beautiful than something harder to accept as beautiful.

Thankfully, I've been feeling well. Cancer is a very funny disease. You can have a cold and not be able to get out of bed, and you can have cancer and do just about everything.

But cancer is also very serious, and sometimes "Mommy's not feeling well." The way I look at it, though, I'm really no different from anyone else. No one knows what's around the corner. We all pray that it should be something good and easily recognizable as beautiful. But who knows what tomorrow will bring?

That's how I deal with the children. I haven't said to them, "Cancer can be fatal," although there are people on the block that have died from cancer and they know it. They have me around today and I'm thankful I can be a mother to them.

Tomorrow is another story — and it would be, even if I didn't have cancer.

My children are eight, six, almost four, and two. It's not easy. In fact, it's incredibly difficult. There have been moments of anger. I've never been able to come out and say, "Thank You, God, for giving me cancer." That's a tough one. I've tried to be very, very real with my anger and not to push it back down. I've tried to really face it head-on.

And I've found that when I accept the anger, it becomes less of an enemy. The same with the fear. Sometimes I have to say, "Okay, I'm scared." But I'm not going to let that fear get the better of me.

I wasn't like this three years ago. I'm two generations from the Holocaust. My grandparents lost almost their entire families. For many years I was angry with God. My relationship was not one of love; it was one of fear. My kids would say, "Mommy, when I'm ten...," and I would think, *God willing, you should live to be ten.* I wasn't the most positive person. I wouldn't say those words, but I would certainly think them.

I've grown since then. When I thank God for the little things, it helps me know that He is with me for the big things. I thank Him for my food and my arms and my legs, and when I go to the hospital, though it's the last place in the world I want to be, I thank Him for that, too. I know He's there with me.

I try to take pleasure in the good instead of focusing on the bad. When I walk in for chemotherapy and the nurse smiles at me, I try to take pleasure in that. She could greet me with a scowl on her face and make the whole experience a lot worse.

Life is like a train ride. The nice thing about this train ride is that everyone has first-class tickets. But we often see people, even ourselves, riding third class. Why is that? Circumstance is never the problem. It's what we conjure up in our imagination that really hurts us. Often the physical pain and the emotional anguish are relatively easy to deal with, but we torment ourselves with worry and fear. Herein lies my challenge. Cancer is not a third-class ticket. Cancer is a guidebook to what first-class has to offer.

Life is beautiful. Let's make it eternally beautiful. And really enjoy.

Appendix B

Excerpts from the Shivah Book

Dear Shaul,

...There are many lessons I've learned, about appreciating life and focusing on others, but I'll close with some memories. My clearest memories are of the period surrounding your wedding — it was such an exciting time for us (Elana's cousins). She was the first to get married — and you brought a certain excitement and craziness to the family. It was such a happy and exciting time! Do you remember how the photographer would prompt everybody to laugh by calling out: "Pretend you're happy with the *shidduch*," and you laughed, and Elana laughed, and we all laughed...

May Hashem bless you and your children with all the best, and may you (we) be comforted amongst the other mourners of Zion and Yerushalayim.

*F. G. (cousin)**

* Names have been changed to retain privacy.

***

Dear Shaul,

I have only known you all, as a family, for a very short time, and yet it seems I have known you forever.

It was an honor to touch the life of Elana, or rather to have her touch my life, which can never be the same again because of that touch.

I found her to be a woman of strength and integrity, full of love and always showing concern for others — rather than centering on herself (which is amazing under the circumstances).

I remember one instance when she called someone to come over so she could ask him to finance a private operation for someone else. When that person arrived, Elana decided it was not the right time to ask him, and she would have to think of another way. What wisdom and generosity for someone so ill to see to the needs of others!

She told me one day what a special husband God blessed her with, and children who are precious. She said she had known a special kind of love and that she did not want to leave.

Thank you, Shaul, for allowing me into your home to have an experience that I will always hold precious. Thank you also for writing "Light in the Darkness" [an article I wrote for Aish.com, the essence of which is contained within this book], which I have shared with others.

I will always remember her laughter in pain, her joy in sickness, and her strength in all she had to face; but you, your love, made it all possible.

Ruth Ann (nurse)

***

Elana was the most special person you could hope to have as an aunt. She really cared about everyone more than she cared about herself. I won't forget when she was sitting and breathing through an oxygen tank, and I told her about my degree results, she said it really made her hour — and it really did!

Thank you for being so special.

L.

***

Dear Shaul and family,

We were privileged to meet Elana about two years ago, and I personally have so much to be grateful for, as indeed does my wife and family.

We were not yet married, and Rachelle was skeptical of religion and of agreeing to have a "traditional" Jewish wedding. She believed people talked down to her and could not empathize with her.

It is wholly true to say that meeting both Elana and Shaul changed that for Rachelle. Finally, Rachelle embraced Judaism and told me after our wedding that it was the first time she felt proud to be Jewish. I have no doubt that this was due to Elana and yourself.

"We live by what we get to survive, but we really live by what we give."

Marvin and Rachelle

***

To all the family,

Elana was an amazing woman. We shared many Shabbats with her and the family, and not only did she cook and set the table and serve the food, she then came and sat and discussed deep subjects as if she had been involved in the conversation from the beginning of the meal!

You never had the impression she was ill, and she always radiated a bright, understanding manner. She was a deeply spiritual person who excelled at the practicalities of life, as well.

This was my memory of Elana.

With much love to you all,
Marcia Freedman

***

Dear Shaul and family,

Elana was such a warm and caring individual — I feel privileged to have known her. Her words of wisdom before my wedding day will always be with me.

She was such an easy person to talk to; she never judged me on my religious level. She made me feel welcome when I first moved to London, and let me stay with her family while I was helping at Aish.

I remember being with her in the hospital on Friday night and helping her light candles for Shabbat.

We chatted as much as we could, and I felt very lucky that she had asked me to help her bring in Shabbat that night.

Love,
Lori and Phillip Morris

***

...To sit and write about all of Elana's qualities would take a very long time. Elana was special to me for a number of reasons. Firstly, because we were fortunate enough to have Shaul perform our wedding ceremony, and any apprehensions I had were eased by Elana. She was a wonderful teacher and made the whole process easier.

Secondly, I found it amazing — the strength and courage that she had. She once told me that she was a quiet, negative person before she had cancer (I never knew her then, so I can't comment) and that cancer had given her the strength and confidence to go and help others. In the talk she gave, "Isn't Life Beautiful?" the thing she said that will always stay in my mind is that everyone in life is given a first class ticket, but most us choose to travel third class. How true is that!

Elana, I want you to know that thanks to you, I wake up every day and ride first class.

She truly was a wonderful person and I really will miss her.

Lucy Stern

❊❊❊

Dear Family,

Elana's trust in Hashem was inspirational. I am sure that in addition to me, many thousands of people will be inspired to put their trust in Hashem and be able to say: "Everything you get is perfect for you."

Jeffrey Feldman

❊❊❊

…I first met Elana when I came to learn *Pirkei Avot* in your flat in Golders Green — sitting on the sofa with Elana, just after Akiva was born. I remember that learning with her was a very warm experience. I really enjoyed being in her company. It was fun as well as stimulating. I didn't see her again until one and a half years ago, when we gathered at the JLE to say *Tehillim* for her. There were about two hundred women there, and to everyone's surprise, Elana herself appeared and spoke to us. She was really amazing and I remember she said, "I can deal with what is happening to me."

The entire room was overwhelmed with her courage. Her words were so powerful; we were all on the verge of tears. Elana was a very brave woman. I will try to carry some of her strength with me.

May you have a long and good life,
Roslynn and Jeremy Green and Baby Jill

***

Dear Family Rosenblatt,

When we moved onto the street, four years ago, Elana was the first one to come to us with flowers and welcome us. Then Yom Kippur came and I was all alone at home, thinking of the holy day and not being able to go to shul or even talk to anyone besides my six-month-old baby. There was a knock at the door and Elana came in with Akiva, Shifra, and Elkana, who was just walking. She stayed for a couple of hours, just to watch my baby so I could daven. I'll always be grateful for that. May you all have a long life.

Hamakom yenachem eschem b'soch she'ar aveilei Tzion v'Yerushalayim.

Esther Cooper

***

To Family Rosenblatt,

An episode I'd like to share with you: I was here one morning about eight weeks before Elana passed away. She suddenly remembered that when she'd sent her daughter off to school that morning, the child had complained of feeling unwell, and she'd promised her that she'd phone the school later on to see how she was doing. Elana phoned the school office and was told that they'd not heard from her daughter, so she should assume that she was fine. But Elana requested that a member of the office staff please go to her daughter and tell her that she had phoned. She said she had to make sure to keep her daughter's trust in her.

R. *Freedenberg*

***

...Such a wonderful person, who shouldn't be remembered just for the last few months, but for everything she achieved in her short lifetime: her friendliness, her abilities, her *kochos*, the way she supported Shaul and the wonderful open home she established —

these are all attributes that mustn't be forgotten. I told Shaul of the hard time she gave me when she thought (mistakenly!) that I was criticizing her husband.

We don't have enough people like Elana that we can afford to lose someone so special. May her *neshamah* be a *melitzas yosher* for her family and for all of us.

R. Baumgarten

***

Dear Shaul and family,

Devorah showed me a letter today that said that to know Elana was a true privilege, and I feel that way, too. I did not know her well, but each time I met her, over the past few years, it struck me that she was always *b'simchah*, radiating a true sense of joy and *ahavas Hashem.*

A story that my brother-in-law told me several weeks ago has stayed in my head and I hope that by sharing it with you, you may find some comfort. He told me that before he became religious — before he began his journey for real — he came to you for a meal. He said that the atmosphere at the table — and in the family as a whole — was something he had never experienced before. He knew then that he wanted to have a family like that.

Baruch Hashem, he is now happily married and, God willing, about to start a family of his own.

The influence that Elana had on everyone she met was tremendous, and I thank Hashem that I was *zocheh* to have the opportunity to meet her, too.

Hamakom yenachem eschem b'soch she'ar aveilei Tzion v'Yerushalayim.

Daniella

***

Dear Shaul and family,

Elana was one in a million; she made people feel instantly at ease and welcome. She was someone to admire, to love, to look up to… She had a great sense of humor.

Together, you have welcomed both Bill and I and many more into your home with open arms — you made us feel part of a community.

I'll never forget the weekly nights, just before we got married, of learning with Elana and just chatting. I used to look forward to it and to the Friday night meals, seders, and other special times we were invited to.

There is so much to say that I could go on and on, but I just want you to know that Elana and you have made a difference to our lives.

Love,
Wendy, Bill, and Dani

❊❊❊

Dear Family,

I was involved in the hospital lifts. Elana's sweetness and unpretentiousness always struck me. The last time I saw her, in May, we were waiting in the Royal Free and I asked if she would like me to massage her neck, shoulders, and back. She said it helped a lot and I was very grateful to be able to give to her in this way. I tried to daven for her as I did the massage, to channel something down to her from Hashem.

Hamakom yenachem eschem b'soch she'ar aveilei Tzion v'Yerushalayim.
Mary Foster

❊❊❊

…Elana touched our lives and our street by her presence. She transformed Woodville Road from being a row of individual homes to being one big, caring family. We are now so powerfully bound together that this *zechus* of *achdus* may be a major factor in bringing Mashiach closer.

On a more personal level, Elana was a loving presence in our home. Not only Shani and Dovi felt powerfully bound to her — we all loved, cared for, and admired her. She was always quoted by the children and myself, especially her *hashgachah* stories. We will remember her with love and affection.

The Simon Family

❊❊❊

...I guess we all have to face death sooner or later, ever since Adam made his mistake. There is nothing like death to help us evaluate what is important, true and lasting, and what isn't. Basically, we appear to lose everything when we die: our loved ones, our bodies, our possessions, our world... And what remains apart from a cold, lifeless body, asleep in the dust?

What remains are the impressions we made as we moved through the world. The memories of every single person we met. Elana, you made a wonderful impression on the world. Your *chesed* for everyone privileged to meet you made us all feel loved, all feel special and all that much richer...

Thank you, dear Elana, for all you did for me. You showed me how to bring up children, even though I don't have any yet. You fed me on Shabbat. You tried to find me a *shidduch*, even though you were dying. *Eishet chayil.* You lived for others and I suspect you died for others — for nothing you ever did could have shortened your life. It was for us that your life was shortened. To teach us the meaning of our lives. A *korban tahor.* A pure offering...

We have faith that HaRachaman keeps His faith to those asleep in the dust.

See you soon, please God, when the dead come back to life, when the Mashiach comes, soon in our days, amen.

In the meantime, enjoy Gan Eden.

Freddy

***

...What can I say about Elana? How warm and welcoming she was from the first time I met her? How pleased she was that I took such good care of Shaul in Poland, twice!? How concerned she was about me — as a friend, as a woman, as a Jew? How amazing she was with her fantastic children? How supportive she was as a wife? How giving she was to everyone who crossed her path? Yes, all those things. And wise, courageous, and deep. But the thing that makes me smile the most is how, when we would sit and chat, she would always bemoan, "But why can't I get my kids to go to bed?" And then she'd laugh that warm, light, and loving laugh.

Ariella

***

Dear Shaul and family,

One encounter sticks out in my mind when I think what to write at this time. Some time ago we said *Tehillim* for Elana at the JLE because the situation had taken a difficult turn. There were over one hundred women in the room, and we were united together in a way that only something like this can bring about. As we were saying *Tehillim*, Elana came into the room. Not only did her presence put inspiration and awe into each and everyone of us, but she spoke to us of the *bitachon* one must have in these times. Her strength and *emunah* will inspire me, and I'm sure all of those who were there, for many years to come. I, for one, will never forget her.

Wishing you the same strength and emunah for the future,

Sylvia Kahan

***

To all Elana's family:

It is very difficult to fully describe Elana, *a"h*. She was constantly striving for perfection. I feel privileged to have known her so personally. She was always looking for *hashgachah peratis* in her life — and it was my *hashgachah* that I lived in her home! I came to London to find a job. Elana made her home my home, and I am deeply grateful to her and her family for that.

One major lesson that struck me about Elana was the importance she attached to anything that was important to anyone else. What manifests this lesson so strikingly was when she was diagnosed for the second time. It was the day before I was about to go home for my sister's engagement, and Elana didn't tell me, so as not to upset me. I would never have guessed that something so major had just happened.

When she did eventually tell me, after I had come back, I was shocked. It took me quite some time to come to grips with the news. I realized that she was actually living her *bitachon*, and that was how she remained so calm. I was amazed at how she continued her life, smiling, looking after the children and generally caring for everyone as she always had. Everyone was important to her! She had something so major on her head, but little things, which were trivial in comparison, were important to her if they would bring someone happiness.

Another thing that amazed me and something I would choose to emulate is how she would get up early to daven and then wake up the children.

It is my wish and dream to be able to emulate her *tzidkus* and constant awareness of Hashem and His love for us.

Kol tuv,
Rochel Berger

* * *

For Elana's family,

Yesterday, I was watching the video of our wedding (which was in November of this year) and it was so nice to see Shaul and

Elana in it. My husband and I met through Aish. I was working in the young professional department, a year and a half ago, and Howard had come to Aish to learn. On our wedding video, Shaul and Elana can be seen trying to make us happy. Elana, so sick, was dancing. We're involved in the community here, and we really love being part of what they created; the friendly, nonjudgmental atmosphere, the warmth and love, the motivation and inspiration to keep growing. Please God, we're soon going to have a baby and look forward to bringing it up according to what we've learnt by being part of this community.

Elana had a special way of showing people what life is about — something very rare. Both my mother and mother-in-law came with me, on separate occasions, to hear Elana speak at the center. They heard a young woman telling them how to get more meaning out of life, without feeling they were being told how to live. They heard her explain how Judaism equipped her with the strength she needed. They learned why my husband and I want to live our lives slightly differently from what they had shown us, and I heard them tell others about this amazing young woman. Elana put into practice, in her short life, what most people don't accomplish in a very long one.

We also came for Shabbos, soon after our marriage, and enjoyed being around the table — the children singing and playing.

All this is my attempt to express how I was able to see such a lot of love and strength, and I am one of many, and she didn't even know me so well. I hope you can find some comfort in my words.

Sara Greenman

***

Dear Rosenblatt family,

I am so deeply sorry and feel with you at this tragic time. I needed to say a big thank you to Elana — and now it is too late. So

I will say it to her special family that are left here.

Elana is responsible for every *berachah*, mitzvah, and good deed that I do. If not for her, I would not be here now. It was the first English fellowships — I had come to Israel to see my sister, and I was not yet observant. Elana had all the time in the world for me, and the love and respect that emanated from her when she spoke to me — no one showed me such warmth before. I thought to myself, *If this is what it means to be observant, then that is what I will be! Baruch Hashem,* I am here now. Thank you, Elana. My only regret is that I never told you to your face.

My greatest sympathies,
Judith Goodman

***

Dear Akiva, Shifra, Elkana, and Sora,

I've decided to write to you, because it is as your Ima that I knew Elana best.

We first met a couple of days before Pesach, nearly six-and-a-half years ago, when Family Rosenblatt — Abba, Ima, Akiva (just over three), and Shifra (a few days short of her first birthday) — moved into Woodville Road. How could anyone, and with two small children besides, move into a new home on *erev Pesach*? And she told me she was going to have I don't remember how many people for seder. Frankly, forgive me for saying so, I thought Ima was more than a bit crazy.

Baruch Hashem, it didn't take me long to realize how very wrong I was. Despite the age difference, we hit it off as neighbors, and over the next six years were in constant touch with each other. I cannot tell you how much I learned from Ima — her calmness, her wonderful *middah* of true *tznius*, her *pashtus*, and her total appreciation for what is important in life. And later, when she was ill, we all learned from her wonderful *emunah*, from her courage, from her positive approach to even the toughest *nisyonos*.

As far as I know, Ima had two equally important priorities in her life. The first was as an *eved Hashem* — she only wanted to do what was right in the eyes of HaKadosh Baruch Hu. And that automatically led to the other — her care for Abba and you, her four darling children. Her concern was always for you, that you should live and grow as Torah-true Jewish children. We talked often about school, about friends and influences, about how we wanted our children to behave, to develop good *middos*, and — most importantly of all to Ima — of how you should make a *kiddush Hashem*, because that is really what our life here is all about. And what a *kiddush Hashem* Ima herself made, especially in the last very special six weeks of her life.

I remember when Ima told me that she was ill, on the day after Yom Kippur three years ago. And she said to me: "I want life to carry on as normal."

It did, and your home remained a happy home and an incredibly open home. Ima kept smiling throughout that first evening, giving us all *chizuk*.

So many, many people said to me during the course of those three years, "Is Elana really ill? I saw her the other day doing carpool, going shopping, at parents' evening, looking so good."

She was so grateful to HaKadosh Baruch Hu for being able to do these normal "Ima jobs," the ones the rest of us so often complain about. And she carried on doing them until the last days of her life. None of us who were there will ever forget how she and Abba fetched you, Sora, when you finished at "Aunty Malke's."

You are privileged to have had an extraordinarily special Ima, who faced the ultimate challenge in life and passed with flying colors. Your challenge in life is to grow up in the way that Ima wanted, and thereby keeping her memory alive in the hearts of all who knew and loved her so much.

With all our love,
"Aunty" Renee and the Weinbergers

***

...Although I only had the pleasure of meeting Elana a few times, the occasions I met her stayed with me and created very poignant memories. Only a truly special person could create such a lasting impression in such a short space of time.

One of my fondest memories of Elana is of when I came over to the family for a Shabbos meal. It was almost time to light candles, and, being the awkward vegetarian that I am, I pronounced to Elana upon arrival, "Oops! Forgot to tell you, sorry!" "No problem," was the response. "Let's see what I can make for you." I explained it wasn't necessary to create a special meal for me and that I would be quite contented with vegetables. In true Elana fashion she said, "Let me make you a fresh pot of vegetables that have not been cooked in a meat dish!" Of course, I declined this offer, explaining that I was more than happy with the food already cooked, but in all my years of being a vegetarian, no one has ever offered to put themselves out in this manner.

As far as I am concerned these were the words of a selfless woman. These were the words of a woman who put others' needs before her own, without ever questioning what the outcome would be for her. Altruism is the hardest asset to attain. To Elana, thinking of others came naturally. Elana would always say, "Everyone is special." I agree. Everyone is special, but some people naturally shine — and Elana was one of those people.

Eve Goldman

***

To the Rosenblatts, Ashers, and extended family:

I have so much to thank Hashem for now. The best move the Rebbetzin ever made was to ask me to leave sem this past June. I couldn't understand the reason for not being in Eretz Yisrael; not learning Torah in sem; not being under the intense supervision of Rebbetzin Weinberg. But when I said *Modim* in *minchah* on the day Elana passed away, I had so much to be grateful for. Grateful for the opportunity to have spent every day, for six weeks, in the Rosenblatt house, getting close to the family. Grateful for having heard hours of wisdom from Elana. Grateful for learning about *emunah* and *ahavas Hashem* from a family who were living it day in and day out.

There are a number of things which I learned from Elana that I would like to pass on.

One night we were discussing her amazing children and how fun it was to spend time with them. She sighed, leaned back on her chair, and closed her eyes. Then she smiled and said, "A taste of heaven…" We discussed their innocence, their trusting nature, and the pure joy they bring to the world.

I began to appreciate everything that brings pleasure to my life.

Once I heard Elana recording her words on tape. Of all things, she had had an insight about the *berachah* we say after the bathroom! "Master of the World, who heals all flesh and does wonders."

What was so "wonderful" about this simple act? Elana questioned. And she answered, with absolute clarity, that we are created with such intricate detail in order to have an individual relationship with our Creator, to appreciate the miracle of being able to function normally. Nothing should be taken for granted, even going to the bathroom.

Elana Rosenblatt loved life. She appreciated life. She lived with the constant awareness that Hashem loved her. May these qualities live on through all of us who knew and loved her.

I am always here for all of you.

Betty Silver

✻✻✻

...I have much to thank you all for, because working for Aish changed my life. Through my experience with Fellowships and being constantly surrounded by inspirational people, I realized that I did, after all, believe in God. A surprise to me! Since this realization, I have found that many things in life have taken on so much meaning — and that is all thanks to Shaul and Elana. When I first met Elana, in Israel, I was so excited. I had heard so many wonderful things about her. I clasped her hands and told her this! Being so modest, I don't think she understood my excitement.

I will always remember Elana for her incredible aura — so calm and serene, so beautiful and full of warmth and love.

I am thinking of you all, and I send my love.

Sonia

✻✻✻

...Every month, we have a Rosh Chodesh *shiur* for ladies. After this month's *shiur*, one of the ladies broke down when she thought about Elkana, whom she had the privilege to teach this year in Torah Temimah's nursery. The story she told us was that after Elkana's birthday party in school, he took home a large sack of presents. When asked a few days later if he had opened all his presents immediately, he said: "No. My mummy told me to open only one present a day and to treasure each present like each day." What a special mother Elana was to make such an impression on a little boy of four-and-a-half years old.

I am a close friend of Elana's. She was a source of strength and inspiration to me. A living angel.

T. L.

***

Dearest Elana,

I will start with a long list of beautiful memories:

When I first started learning with Shaul, in 1996, I used to come to the house every Sunday morning. Elana would always serve us tea and cake. Coming from a world which promotes equality, I found it difficult to understand how a woman who was trying to give her children breakfast and organize her house could let her husband sit there teaching, much less serve tea.

It took me a long time to understand that Elana's efforts were not those of a submissive wife, but rather those of a devoted partner in her husband's mission. That she saw the act of serving her husband and guest tea as being as fundamentally significant as whatever wisdom her husband was imparting. In her quiet and subtle way, this was Elana's strength.

I pray that at this difficult time, the family will be strengthened. And that, in the future, the children will be inspired by a mother who was so devoted and so unique in everything she did.

All the best,

Samuel

***

...My memory of Elana is of a sweet, intelligent, and beautiful human being. To me, Elana was a shining star — with not just beauty on the outside but with a beauty that emanated from within. Once, when I saw Elana, she said, "Anna Lehrer, I like you and I really want to start a friendship with you!"

My response was, "I'm so sorry I haven't been in touch, but I've been having a lot of problems in my life and I didn't want to burden you with them when you have so many difficulties going on in you own life."

In true Elana fashion, her response was, "Anna — burden me;

that's what I'm here for. A problem shared is always a problem halved."

To me these were the words of a truly good, kind, and loving person.

I hope as a family you can take solace from knowing that Elana is now in a better place and truly at peace.

May it comfort you all to know that others are with you at this very sad time.

With much love and affection,
Anna Lehrer

***

...My beautiful, sweet sister-in-law. Always so calm, serene, pure, and true. I can't believe she's not here, but I know that she really is here with Shaul and the children, always watching over them.

The last conversation she was able to have with me, only a few days before she passed away, was when someone made a joke at someone else's expense and she struggled to say, "I'm trying not to hear any *lashon hara*." That is the lesson that I am going to take from Elana. I am going to try, *bli neder*, to stop speaking and hearing *lashon hara*. It's not easy. It's one of the most difficult challenges, but I'm going to try in Elana's merit.

During the last days of her illness, the first words she said to me after struggling for breath for ten minutes were, "Hashem has been so good to me."

I will always love and respect her.

Mal

***

To a wonderful family,

My memories of Elana are her soft smile and soft-spoken nature. Elkana was in my kindergarten for the past year. Our only concern was that he was a little quiet, sometimes too quiet. Elkana always had a happy disposition. He is a gorgeous child. My team and I marveled at how well-adjusted and well-balanced he is. We could never have known from him what was happening at home. The credit is definitely due to all of you: Shaul and Elana's parents and Chana and all those involved in caring for and loving Elkana. It is a very big deal that there were no behavioral problems to monitor. We were all moved immensely when Elana made that tremendous effort to attend Elkana's graduation. I have no more words — may Hashem bless you all with tremendous courage and strength.

Shanah Reef (head of kindergarten)

***

To all the Rosenblatts:

I had the *zechus* of being able to come and give Elana massages during the last few months of her time here with us, and each time was a joy and a great learning experience for me. She brought me closer to God by her words, her joy and strength, and her powerful *bitachon.* The day after Elana passed away, I had an interview at Chai Lifeline. The interview took place as Elana was being buried in Eretz Yisrael. I spoke briefly to the receptionist and it came up that I knew Elana and had helped her be more comfortable towards the end. The receptionist was deeply moved and said that the whole organization had valued tremendously every contact they had with her.

She told the interviewer about my connection to Elana, and we spent a great deal of time talking about Elana and her family. In the end, they offered me a job on the merit of my contact with Elana — even though my qualifications weren't "officially" high enough.

I sat there thinking that a tzaddik truly lives forever. For even as Elana was being laid to rest, her goodness continued to radiate on those of us who came into contact with her.

May Hashem give you all comfort to continue in her footsteps, that we should merit to see her again with the coming of Mashiach.

Barbara May Diamond

***

Dear Shaul and Family,

I rang your home on the day Elana had her final scan. She had just heard the worst. Unknowingly, I asked how she was. She said that she was okay. We chatted for a while.

She called me later to apologize. She had forgotten to tell me about an event at Aish that she thought I'd enjoy.

By this time, I had found out about the scan. I tried to imagine the thoughts that another person would have in the same situation.

Elana, you are unique. You would be an example to me if I thought that I could even begin to emulate your ways. You have guided me, fed me, lent me your house. Now you have left, but I am changed.

Thank you, thank you, thank you.

Marc and Penina

***

There are many memories of Elana, but two stand out the most. The first is the Rosenblatt Purim *seudah* of 2001. I remember being extremely moved by Elana's smile, warmth, and endless giving to us, her guests, considering the adverse conditions she had to cope with. Considering some severely boisterous behavior, broken wedding china, and a seriously bruised husband, on top of the pain of her condition, it was clear to me that Elana's giving was totally boundless. It was as if it was unthinkable for her not to be providing for her guests in every possible way.

The other memory is of a regular Shabbos, maybe six or seven months ago, which for me exemplified her strength and courage. Elana had come to shul at Aish, and I remember reacting with concern when I heard she was in the building, not knowing what to expect. I was truly amazed to see Elana at Kiddush with a happy face, talking with everyone who wanted to speak, not imposing herself on them, but genuinely caring about them. To me this was more than a "brave face." It was the real, deep, beautiful nature of a totally unique individual.

One in a million is too small a ratio.

Love,
Sidney

❋❋❋

…I remember you and Elana opening your wedding presents. Elana wanted to save all the beautiful cards, so that she could thank everyone, not only for the gift, but for the card as well.

Devora

❋❋❋

Elana was my "sister." She quickly became a very loved and valued member of the Rosenblatt family. It was a standing joke between us on my visits that if she said Shaul was out or busy, I would say that I came to see her and the children, not my brother!

She rang me to share Akiva's year 4 optional SATS results, and she was just so proud of his achievement.

She was always so calm and serene, no matter what chaos was going on around her.

Almost the last words she said to me on July 20th were, "Why so *frum*?" Even though she was very tired, she still noticed that I was wearing a long skirt and a shirt with long sleeves. This was not my normal mode of dress. Trust my Elana to have noticed. Even though she always accepted me and my way of life, I am so glad I was "properly" dressed the last time we saw each other.

She will always hold a special place in my heart and I value the things she has taught my family.

With all my love,
Sue

***

...So many memories of Elana.

One especially sticks out in my mind — it happened this past Pesach, in Israel. We were having difficulties making the travel plans for the return trip back to England. It was possible that there wouldn't be enough space for the whole entourage. I said, "Are you worried?" And she replied, "I used to worry about things like that." The whole week she was here, it was obvious she didn't feel well — but she didn't complain once. She made sure her kids' and husband's needs were taken care of, and often forgot about her own. A true living example of what a Jewish woman should be. Such an honor and privilege to be in her presence.

Rachelle Heyer

***

Dearest Shaul and all of your beautiful family,

I can't thank you enough for my foundation in *Yiddishkeit*, my vision of who I could be, and for the continuing source of support you gave to me through all of my now-seemingly-petty dramas. You always made me feel important. Shaul, you always said to me, when I called to ask if I could come for Shabbos (usually at around 11:00 p.m. on Thursday night), "Elana will be so happy." I was always so relieved; you were my retreat, my home-away-from-home, my escape from insanity…everything.

Elana always took me seriously, even at my most stupid times. She would smile at me and say, "Frannie, you know what you need to do." It was this absolute *yashrus* that kept me straight, because she was right — I did deep down always know what to do. Thank you, thank you, thank you, for being the most real and powerful role models. All of you are in my thoughts constantly. Hashem should bless you with inner strength as well as outer.

All my love,
Fran

***

At Elana and Shaul's wedding, in the midst of all the joyous celebrations, Shaul said, "Elana wants to know what she should call you." I said, "Let her call us Sonia and Max. That seems to be the modern way." But Elana said, "No!" She wanted to call us Mum and Dad. We were so touched, and that was the beginning of a close and loving relationship with our new daughter.

We both loved Shaul and shared our pride in his achievements. She would say, "He's your son." And I would say, "But he's your husband," because, as his mother, I knew she was his inspiration.

She was a very, very special girl and I will always think about her and love and miss her.

Sonia Rosenblatt

Appendix C

Excerpts from the Sheloshim Speeches

RABBI NOACH ORLOWEK

There is a concept in Judaism called *eis ratzon*, a time of Divine favor. When a person stands under the *chuppah* it's an *eis ratzon*. It's a time when Hashem shows an inclination to be closer. This doesn't mean that Hashem has moods; it means that the glass is thinner. On Rosh HaShanah and Yom Kippur the glass is thinner. It's easier to see things; it's an opportunity. When a baby cries at a bris, it's a moment when you can join in, a time when your prayers are more easily heard. When the Torah is taken out, on Shabbos and even on a Monday and Thursday, it's a time to ask for help because the glass is thinner.

The Gemara says about the funeral of Rabbi Yehudah HaNasi:

"Whoever is at Rebbe's funeral is invited to *Olam HaBa*." What does this mean? There's a spiritual rule that you don't get something for nothing. Did being at Rabbi Yehudah HaNasi's funeral grant one a ticket to *Olam HaBa*?

The Gemara says in *Moed Katan*: "*Misas tzaddikim mechaperes* — the death of the righteous is an atonement." How does someone else dying act as a *kapparah* for me? The answer, Rabbi Dessler says, is that I'm supposed to be touched. I'm supposed to feel something. It's an opportunity.

The Gemara says that when you say good-bye to somebody you should be careful with what you say. Why? Because when you leave someone you become precious to them and whatever you say will be remembered. He appreciates you because he's losing you.

A funeral is an opportunity to catch on to something, to latch onto something. It's like a train pulling out; as you run to catch it, you have to appreciate it…

RABBI JAMIE COWLAND

About four months ago my wife and I experienced a dramatic change in our life. It was a Wednesday and we were at work at the London Aish office when my wife received a call from Elana asking her to be her *chavrusa* for *cheshbon hanefesh*. By that point Elana was very weak, but she was determined to start. And she insisted that she come to our house and that my wife not come over to her. At around 10:00 that night I went upstairs, while downstairs they got to work on a whole *cheshbon* — what they were going to focus on, what they were going to do...

Later, I came downstairs to see if everything was okay and I remember Elana being so full of intensity. Then all of a sudden she was filled with complete exhaustion and said, "I have to go home."

We arranged for her to go home at once, but my life and the life of my wife pretty much changed after that. From that day on my wife spent about an hour to an hour and a half with Elana every day, working on their *cheshbon hanefesh.* She would bring those insights home and we would talk about them.

I just want to share a few things we learned from Elana, and I hope everyone else can learn them, too.

The awareness that my wife and Elana were working on was trying to feel Hashem being with them all the time. My wife told me that by the end she felt that Elana did not need to do any more work on it. It was absolutely constant with her, constant and deep. We felt a little dwarfed by that. My wife kept on trying and they learned more and deeper ideas on this subject, but she felt that Elana had reached a *shleimus* where she didn't feel any sense of self. My wife kept telling me that Elana just wanted to feel Hashem and to be *bateil* to that, to be a *kli* for that, and that she was pushing and pushing herself, despite a tremendous amount of pain and many other issues and problems in her life. She just wanted to be *bateil* and *mevutal.*

I remember when I first joined the London branch of Aish HaTorah. It was the day after I had received *semichah*, on Taanis Esther a few years ago. I flew to England on the fourteenth of Adar and went straight to Shaul's house for the Purim *seudah.* As usual, there were a few hundred people running in and out of the house and Shaul was jumping on some garbage cans outside, if I remember correctly, and this *tzadeikes* was in the middle of it all with a smile on her face. No one else could have smiled on a day like that, I'm sure of it. But you could come into their home as a new person in the branch or as a person unconnected to Judaism or as the *frummest* person in the community and you never felt any sense of imposition, no matter what time it was. I think there are more people in Golders Green that know the combination to the Rosenblatts' front door and the burglar alarm number than their own telephone number. People get calls all the time — "I've just walked into the Rosenblatts, the alarm's going off, what's the number?" It happened to me two days ago, three days ago...

Elana never imposed herself on anybody and you never felt anything was too much trouble. There was always kindness and softness and patience whenever you called, whenever you walked in. I would come for meetings with Shaul, and Elana would always say, "Can I bring you a drink?" She would never think of keeping you downstairs while she made the drink; you were expected to go upstairs to Shaul's study, and a few minutes later a hot drink would be in your hand. It was always about you and never, never, at least in my experience, about herself.

And the thing that impacted me the most powerfully of all was her care for *klal Yisrael.* I remember when we were just starting out in the branch, we had these Friday night events that were held two hours away from us. Shaul would always be at those Friday nights, sometimes with Elana, sometimes without Elana. Shaul would come on Fellowships programs in Israel for a week or two, sometimes with Elana, sometimes without. There was a complete focus on *mesirus nefesh* and, at the same time, on maintaining a tremendous sense of home. A Jewish home. A really Jewish home, despite all the strains and stresses of the type of work we are doing. It never faltered, it was anchored so deeply. There was a tremendous sense of *mesirus nefesh. Mesirus nefesh* in terms of herself — she wanted to be *bateil* and *muvetal. Mesirus nefesh* in terms of others — you never felt there was anything in the world but your needs and the needs of *klal Yisrael.* They came first. Do the right, do the right thing.

Elana even started teaching. She didn't want to teach, but people wanted to hear, so she taught.

My wife should really be the one speaking now, because she knew her best. I only know about Elana second-hand, when my wife would come home and talk about the insights she had gained from Elana, how she grew, how she changed. My wife explained as follows: We understand that there's a Ribbono shel Olam. We understand that there's a finite world. We are drawn towards our finiteness and we have to push ourselves away from our finiteness towards infinity. A move away from self is a move towards self.

The one thing Elana exemplified is this concept that a move away from self is a move towards self. The more you are willing to be *moser nefesh*, the more you are willing to be *mevatel* yourself, the more you are willing to throw caution into the winds and give unconditionally because you see that Hashem has put *hashgachah* in front of you, regardless of your own needs, just to give and give, endlessly, the more you get in touch with yourself.

We have a craziness about this, in my opinion. We think that by investing in ourselves we are investing in ourselves. This is a mistake, and it's a legacy that Elana has left for us.

Whenever I went in to see Elana, and she was very ill at the end, I would say, "How are you doing?" and she would lift herself up and sit straighter. The last time I ever spoke to her, I said, "How are you doing?" and she said, "Fantastic!" with a big smile and held both arms up in the air, in a victory signal. She said that because there was no way she was going to get me involved. She had no sense of self.

I hope that you can learn from this that a move away from self is a move towards self.

RABBI NOAH WEINBERG

We're talking about Elana Golda, and everyone knows so much about her. The fact that she decided to leave public school and go learn Torah in a strange environment when she was twelve years old tells us something about her. The fact that when she was eighteen she joined us as a *madrichah* on Discovery tells us a little more. Shaul asked me to meet her before they got engaged, and I told him that she was one in a million — and I haven't met a million. That tells us a little more. But I didn't really know Elana till she got sick.

To tell you the essence of what I learned about her, I need to quote a *midrash*: "*Amar Rebbe*...in the World to Come, everyone is going to stand in astonishment and wonder at the one who listened to the Almighty." They will say, "Who is this? He's a nobody. He doesn't have Torah knowledge, he never learned a mishnah and yet he's sitting and conversing with the *avos* of this world — Avraham, Yitzchak, and Yaakov!"

The Almighty will explain, "*Mipnei mah zachu eilu mei'eilu?*" What is it made our *avos* the patriarchs of the world? And our *imahos*? What did they do? "They really listened to Me."

When Elana got sick, that's when I really got to know her. Whenever I visited she wanted to ask me questions about her sickness, how to live with it, how to respond to it. How to keep her trust in life and how to react to the Almighty. And she was listening, all the time trying to understand how to live with joy when looking at the children she was going to be parted from. How do you take pain? And how do you remember that the Almighty loves you when struggling for breath? She was listening for answers.

Before she died Elana wrote letters to her children, to her husband, to her mother, to her father, to her brother, and to far-off cousins. Somebody told me that she wrote to a cousin who was in danger of intermarriage, "Please don't do it! I want you to know that if you marry out I will come back and haunt you..."

For English people that is particularly threatening!

Elana didn't write me a letter, but she sent me a message with one of the people who were with her. She said to tell me that she finally understood what I meant by the fact that the Almighty loves us and the Almighty loves her. She felt the Almighty's love. She really listened to God. She heard him. I know that now she's sitting there talking to our fathers, Avraham, Yitzchak, and Yaakov.

RABBI SHAUL ROSENBLATT

"A*shirah laHashem ki gamal alai* — I will sing to the Almighty because He has bestowed of His goodness upon me." This is always what I thought of when I thought of Elana. And I feel the same when I think of her today. Most people knew Elana through her illness. There is no question that her illness lifted her to levels that I can only dream of. But I knew she was a very special person from the day I met her.

Therefore, I would rather speak about how she was when she was well than how she was when she was ill.

I was reading some of the letters that we sent to each other when we were dating, and some of the notes I wrote in a diary I kept then. I couldn't believe she was for real. I didn't believe a girl like this existed in my generation. I just kept pinching myself — is this really who she is?

So I took her to the *rosh yeshivah*, Rav Noah. I wanted to check. And the *rosh yeshivah* said that she was one in a million. I figured, well, there are twelve million Jews in the world. That makes six million women. So if Elana is one in a million, that means there are six such women in this generation. I figured, even if she was number six on the list, I sure wasn't going to go looking for the top five!

But I still wanted to be sure, so I could believe it. I took her handwriting to a few experts and they all confirmed what I already knew. She really was the amazing human being I perceived her to be.

After she passed away, we got a lot of notes from people, lots of condolence letters… My in-laws got one from a friend of theirs, sharing a memory of Elana. They remembered Elana at four years old, davening in shul. They said that their memory of her childhood sincerity and innocence affects them to this day.

But really, there were four reasons why I married Elana. The first was her commitment to *klal Yisrael*; the Jewish people was her greatest passion in life. I often find at Aish — and I am guilty of this myself — that we sometimes lose sight of the trees for the forest. You've got a whole, big *klal Yisrael* that you are trying to affect, and it's easy to lose sight of the individuals. But Elana never did. To her, every Jew mattered. Every Jew was special. She understood that while we may be looking at the big picture, the small picture is important as well.

We had an Israeli in our street who lived four doors down. He was not involved in the Jewish community and didn't want to be. So I didn't waste my time. But Elana always made sure to knock on his door and speak to him. She'd always send him *mishloach manos* on Purim and try to help him make a connection to something Jewish.

Her second strength was her commitment to truth, her determination to change when she saw the truth. I wanted to quote the same *midrash* that the *rosh yeshivah* just quoted — I feel that that's who she was. She wanted to do what was right. She wanted to do the *ratzon Hashem* all her life.

A Kabbalist in London, who didn't know me or Elana, who called me in to see him after Elana passed away. He said that he'd never said this about anyone else before, but he felt Elana's *neshamah* is sitting with the *imahos*, with our matriarchs, Sarah, Rivkah, Rachel, and Leah. Now whether you are into Kabbalists or not, I don't know, and I'm not particularly into them myself, but one thing I do know is that you wouldn't say such a thing about me.

I looked in Elana's diary after she passed away, and she had a list of her roles. Roles that she felt she had to live up to in this world. Her number-three role, her third priority in life, was her role as a mother. Now, don't let the fact that it was her third priority take away from her success as a mother. Just look at our children, and you'll see what a wonderful mother she was. Her number-two role was as a wife. No matter how committed she was to our children, I always came first. But her number-one role, the purpose she held above all else, was to be an *eved Hashem*. She wanted to serve the Almighty. That's all that really mattered in her life.

The third strength Elana had was the way she gave and gave to everyone — Jew and non-Jew alike. Many a time I would come home and find her giving advice to our Romanian cleaning lady, either about her relationship with her boyfriend or about how she missed her family in Romania. Elana had time for everybody. After Elana passed away, this cleaning lady said to me that she looked to Elana like a mother. We had a nurse who looked after Elana just during the last two weeks of her life, a non-Jewish woman called Ruth. She was fifty-two years old, a black, Pentecostal Christian. Elana found out that she wasn't married and asked anyone who came in, "Do you know a Boaz for our Ruth?" She was dying, but she really wanted to find someone for her nurse.

I could go on all night giving examples of Elana's care for others, but I'll just tell a few more stories. When Elana was diagnosed with a recurrence of cancer, about eighteen months ago, the doctors, who had painted a bleak picture from the very start, painted it even bleaker. We came back from the doctor's visit together, and we were both very distraught and upset. At that time, we had a girl from Gateshead living with us to help out. Her name was Rochel. Before we walked into the house, Elana reminded me that this girl's brother was getting married in a few days, and we shouldn't allow our pain to ruin her *simchah*. "We can't let on that we heard bad news. We have to keep it a secret until she goes away," said Elana. And so, for the next few days, I had to put on a show along with Elana. We had to pretend that nothing was the matter. Later, Rochel said she couldn't believe that we were able to do this. She wouldn't have known that anything was wrong. And Elana did it all just so that Rochel could enjoy her *simchah* without feeling our pain.

And one last story, which I hope will not get me into trouble — when she was giving birth, at the height of the pain, she would always say, "Don't worry. I know that this harder for you than it is for me. I'm not in that much pain. Please don't be worried. I'm doing just fine." Even when she was in incredible pain, she was only thinking of me and how I was feeling.

The way she gave and gave was the third reason that I married her.

But the fourth, and final, reason — and to me it was the most important thing I was looking for in a wife — was her *tznius*. Elana was a true *bas Yisrael*, and *tznius* was her greatest *middah*. For Elana, it wasn't just the way she dressed, it would resonate in everything she did. *Tznius* was about her children, her house, how she shopped, how she walked down the street, how she spoke on the phone. To her, *tznius* was all of life.

Not long before she passed away, Elana asked for a tape so that she could record something. I was surprised because she didn't really have the energy to speak. But she desperately wanted to speak about *tznius* and with her almost final breath she left a message to our daughters. She said *tznius* isn't just about how long your skirt is or how long your sleeves are — although that's part of it. *Tznius* is how you are as a person. Who are you dressing for? Are you dressing for the world or to be an *eved Hashem*? That, to her, was what *tznius* was all about. And she always dressed, and acted, to be an *eved Hashem*. To her, *tznius* wasn't a list of restrictions but rather a complete and beautiful guide to *avodas Hashem*.

A spouse is an incredible gift. In the last three years, from the time Elana got sick, we attained a oneness that was previously unimaginable. I look back and feel that there are times when I didn't appreciate her and I wish I had. There are times when I didn't give enough and I wish I had. I don't feel guilty, but I feel a sense of regret. And I say to those who are married and to those who are going to get married: Don't leave room for regrets. Don't wait to lose that which you love.

A spouse is one of the most beautiful, wonderful gifts you will get in your life. Go home tonight and appreciate and love and give and spend time together. Look your spouse in the eyes and say again and again how wonderful you think he or she is. Break out of the self-centered pettiness that often creeps into close relationships. Life is too short for that. Love the person you love and do it with all that you have.

To quote Elana: When you have a disagreement, when you have a problem in a relationship, don't focus on winning the argument; focus on winning the relationship.

I just want to finish with some "thank you's." First, I would like to thank my in-laws for raising such a wonderful girl and for all your support over the last three years and especially in the past three months.

I would also like to thank my own parents for accepting and loving Elana as a daughter. Even though you were thousands of miles away, I've been strengthened by your support.

I want to say thank you to the whole Aish family, here and worldwide. The support has just been incredible.

I want to thank my rebbe, the *rosh yeshivah*. I could say thank you all night to my rebbe, the *rosh yeshivah*, for giving me life, but specifically for flying in so many times and giving us your *hashkafah* and guidance. You blazed a bright path through what could have been such a dark time. Elana and I grew so deeply from your clarity. Without it, this would have been impossible. And I want to say thank you to the *rebbetzin*, who has given both Elana and me and Elana's family such good advice. You came at just the right time and knew just what Elana needed to hear. In the last few weeks, Elana grew to levels that I've never experienced in a human being. I'm confident that it was due mainly to the time that you, Rebbetzin, spent with her.

I want to thank you, Elana my dear. Thank you for twelve wonderful years. Thank you for four beautiful children. Thank you for never judging me...for always loving me...for fighting till your very last breath to stay with me and the children. Thank you for taking a boy and turning him into a man. I look forward to sharing eternity with you. Please save me a place!

Finally, a thank You to Hashem. Thank you for twelve special years with the most beautiful wife in the world. Thank you for giving her cancer. It was painful. It was horrific. But both she and I knew and know that it was worth it — so worth it. Cancer gave us so much more than it took away. Thank You, Hashem. Please send the *geulah* soon so that we can see our Elana once more...

THANK YOU

To the Golders Green / Hendon Community

During the past 3 years of Elana's ע"ה illness and subsequent petirah, we have been overwhelmed with the chesed and love of the Jewish community.

The community has been everything we have needed it to be and a true Kiddush Hashem.

We came to England 8 years ago to give of ourselves, but what we have received in return has been many times more than we have given.

So many people have helped that it is difficult to thank everyone personally. Please accept this as a personal thank you to those who looked after our children, cooked for us, drove Elana to and from hospital, visited her and cared for her, picked up medicines, organized tehillim, inquired about our wellbeing, thought about us and davened for us.

It has been a challenging 3 years. Hashem always sends the refuah before the makka and the Golders Green / Hendon community was part of our refuah. Refuah does not always come in the way we ask for it and such is the case here. But Hashem is our Father who always gives us just what we need. We thank Him for His incredible goodness.

We wish the whole community a kesiva v'chasima tova.

מִי שֶׁבֵּרַךְ אֲבוֹתֵינוּ אַבְרָהָם יִצְחָק וְיַעֲקֹב, הוּא יְבָרֵךְ אֶת
כָּל הַקָּהָל הַקָּדוֹשׁ הַזֶּה, עִם כָּל קְהִלּוֹת הַקֹּדֶשׁ,
הֵם, וּנְשֵׁיהֶם, וּבְנֵיהֶם, וּבְנוֹתֵיהֶם, וְכָל אֲשֶׁר לָהֶם.

With great appreciation

The Rosenblatt and Asher Families

A half-page notice that we placed in the local Jewish newspaper during Elana's sheloshim.

GLOSSARY

Abba — father, daddy

achdus — unity

afikoman — the last piece of matzah eaten at the seder

a"h — acronym for *aleha hashalom*, may she rest in peace

ahavas Hashem — love of God

Amidah — the silent prayer recited three times a day (also called "*Shemoneh Esrei*")

avos — the patriarchs

baruch Hashem — thank God

bas Yisrael — Jewish girl

bateil — nullified

berachah — blessing

bitachon — trust in God

bitul Torah — neglect of Torah study

bli neder — without promising

BT — acronym for "*baal teshuvah*," one who returns to Judaism *chavrusa* — study partner

chesed — kindness

cheshbon hanefesh — introspection; spiritual self-accounting

chizuk — strength

chuppah — the canopy under which a wedding ceremony takes place, or the wedding ceremony itself

Eishes Chayil — song from Proverbs traditionally sung in Jewish homes on Friday nights; also used to refer to a woman of valor

emunah — faith

Eretz Yisrael — the land of Israel

eved Hashem — servant of God

FFB — acronym for "*frum* from birth," meaning one who was raised as a religious Jew

frum — religious

geulah — redemption

HaKadosh Baruch Hu — God

Hamakom yenachem eschem b'soch she'ar aveilei Tzion v'Yerushalayim — May God comfort you amongst the mourners of Zion and Jerusalem

hashgachah — Divine providence

Ima — mother, mommy

imahos — matriarchs

kapparah — atonement

kiddush Hashem — sanctification of God's name

klal Yisrael — the Jewish nation

kli — vessel

kochos — strengths, spiritual capabilities

kol tov — all the best

lashon hara — evil or derogatory speech

Mashiach — the Messiah

melitzas yosher — advocate (in Heaven)

mesirus nefesh — self-sacrifice

mevatel — to nullify

mevutal — nullified

middah (pl. *middos*) — character trait

middah keneged middah — measure for measure

minchah — the afternoon prayer

mishloach manos — packages of food sent to friends on the holiday of Purim

Modim — a paragraph of thanksgiving to God in the Silent Prayer recited daily

neshamah — soul

nisyonos — tests, challenges

Olam HaBa — the World to Come

pashtus — simplicity

Pirkei Avos — Ethics of the Fathers

ratzon Hashem — the will of God

rebbetzin — the wife of a rabbi; a woman of spiritual stature

Rosh Chodesh — first day of the lunar month

rosh yeshivah — dean of a yeshivah

semichah — rabbinic ordination

seudah — festive meal

Shabbos — the Sabbath

sheloshim — the first thirty days of mourning after a person's death

sheva berachos — the seven blessings recited at a wedding ceremony or the seven days of celebration following a wedding *shidduch* — match, marriage partner

shiur — Torah class

shleimus — completion

simchah — joy; happy occasion

Tehillim — Psalms

tzadeikes — righteous woman

tzidkus — righteousness

tznius — modesty

yashrus — integrity

Yerushalayim — Jerusalem

Yiddishkeit — Judaism

zechus — a merit

zocheh — to merit

z"l — acronym for "*zichrono* (or *zichronah) levrachah*," may his (or her) memory be for a blessing

About the Author

Rabbi Shaul Rosenblatt was born in Liverpool, England, and spent six years studying in Aish HaTorah, Jerusalem. He now lives in London with his wife, Chana, and their six children. He is the founder of Aish HaTorah UK and until recently served as its executive director. He also founded Honestreporting.com. He is now codirector of Tikun, an organization under the auspices of Aish HaTorah whose goal is to show young Jews that Judaism is focused on *tikun hamiddos*, personal development, and *tikun olam*, changing the world.